Dance in West Africa

Ulrike Groß

Dance in West Africa

Analysis and description in relation to aspects of communication theory

Waxmann 2020
Münster · New York

Bibliographic information published by the Deutsche Nationalbibliothek
The Deutsche Nationalbibliothek lists this publication in
the Deutsche Nationalbibliografie; detailed bibliographic data
are available in the Internet at http://dnb.dnb.de

Internationale Hochschulschriften, vol. 673

ISSN 0932-4763
Print-ISBN   978-3-8309-3874-3
E-Book-ISBN 978-3-8309-8874-8

© Waxmann Verlag GmbH, 2020
Steinfurter Straße 555, 48159 Münster

www.waxmann.com
info@waxmann.com

Cover design: Anne Breitenbach, Münster
Typesetting: Stoddart Satz- und Layoutservice, Münster

Printed on age-resistant paper,
acid-free as per ISO 9706

Contents

1.	General introduction	9
2.	What is dance?	12
3.	**Dance and science**	18
3.1	Ethnology	18
3.2	The psychological approach	21
3.3	Historical perspectives	22
3.4	Semiotic, linguistic and phenomenological approaches	23
3.5	African dance as a subject of musicology and ethnology	24
4.	The Ewe	28
5.	The Ewe language	29
6.	**Religion in Ewe Society**	30
7.	**Preconsiderations in Communication Theory**	37
8.	**Comparison of verbal and non-verbal forms of communication**	40
8.1	The visual channel	41
8.2	Confining and containing the object of investigation	44
9.	**Description of a dance-event from a dance-inherent point of view**	46
10.	**Transcription and notation**	48
11.	**Evaluation of the data**	56
11.1	Explanation of material	58
11.2	Evaluation of 'motion data'	60
11.3	Basic movement	62
11.4	Bodily and spatial orientation	63
11.5	Orientation of observers	64
11.6	Establishing the space	69
11.7	Classification of bodily movements	71
11.8	Corporal segmentation, notation and description thereof	72

12. Describing the various positions 74

13. Discussion of dance data 104

14. From gesture to text...106

Glossary of terminology 119

Bibliography 162

1.   General introduction

The following study centres on the subject of dance; specifically, 'African Dance'. The term 'African Dance', as used in other publications and here, is misleading. It gives the impression that there is *one* form of dance in Africa, African Dance. There is no single form of dance in Africa as much as there is no single African language or music.

To put into perspective just how varied the dance landscape is, consider: there are about 2500 languages on the African continent today. We can furthermore assume that dance as a manifestation in Africa is likewise more frequently come across than on the European continent. If one settles on ten dances per linguistic-community, which is minimal given further variations, one would reach a figure of some 25000 dances, each with its own different 'language of movement' and content, with further possible modifications. *There are thus an infinite numbers of dances with an unpredictable number of dance-configurations.*

The term 'African Dance' will be used to describe an activity of varied form and function.

Traditional dances have not, of course, remained unchanged over time. Formerly, they undoubtedly had another meaning. It happened that elements of dance transformed themselves due to contact with outside influences.

The multifunctionality of dance mirrors all facets of life and is a companion and support during important phases of life. It is a means of cultural expression and a reflection of reality.

It is fundamentally:
- a means of communication with an implicit 'linguistic' function
- a means of artistic expression
- expression within a framework of religious ritual
- the expression of a political and social hierarchy within a ceremonial framework
- a means of political expression
- an expressive means of coping with conflict
- a component part of one's upbringing and socialization
- a component in military training
- a means of preventive health care, bodily fitness and healing
- a means of maintaining mental health
- a way of earning a living

One work cannot do justice to the variety and wonders of dance. Selecting the **'Adzogbo'** (dance), from the Ewe of southern Ghana, is an attempt to try, to whatever degree.

I cannot deny that a prime motivation is having a passion and admiration for this type of dance expression. Bibliographic research reveals that, despite the quantity of material and its socio-cultural significance, there is astonishingly little written knowledge in existence, and this, given the volume of data and the value attached to dance in Africa. One perceives that it has been marginalised as a subject of research. With this work, I hope to confront any prevailing prejudices surrounding the integrity of this means of expression.

1. The objectives are to make a narrative of dance and derive a context of movement and movement sequences. This is a new approach. I have found neither evidence of African dance 'narration' nor sequential movement being so clearly described.
   It is thus necessary to embed this form of expression within a communications-theoretical framework.

   This work results in the following derived hypothesis:
   Dance is the 'conversion' of:
   a) musical structures, presented with the help of musicians;
   b) a non-verbal expression of text, as presented via the 'Talking Drum', in place of conventional, spoken expression.
   Westermann covers the aspect thus: "every movement has a generally acknowledged meaning [...], and in this way it is possible to explain whole stories and 'fates' without words [...] the indigenous people name this: speaking through dance. 'He wants to speak through dance'" (Westermann, 1907, 12).

2. Even today we fail to recognise the socio-cultural significance and importance of dance. One assumes that one's own point of view impresses itself upon the way one observes and interprets others. The potential for expression through dance in the context of our daily lives has all but disappeared. It is thus difficult to understand this approach to dance (in other cultures) and to imagine the appreciation in which dance is held.
   It is difficult to accept dance as a part of normal daily practice and expression, as practised by every individual, female or male. Our diktat is the spoken word. We may not reject but rather prefer to overlook the fact that we communicate both verbally and physically. "Speech acts and non-ver-

bal acts, as 2 modes of communication, are inextricably related" (F. Key, 1980, 392).
Christian missionaries were the first and most important researchers of the Ewe. Their ethical and moral viewpoint was that of dance as being a sin. Most missionaries thus tried to suppress dance (Hanna, 1966, 303). One should not, however, denounce their work in hindsight. A detailed chapter considers the very idea of dance, as supported by the church for hundreds of years and tries to work out why the elimination of dance, due to the ethical/moral background of the missionaries, was intended and partially successful. Exchanged letters (of great detail) of the Basel and Bremen missionaries were viewed, evaluated and interpreted.
A further reason for the absence of dance in academic research could be due to the lack of ways of reporting aspects of movement technique.

3. As with speech, dance is an ephemeral phenomenon. It would have been especially difficult for those untrained in movement observation and analysis to note material down. Thus the course of a dance could have been annotated with the use of **"statues"**.
    By evaluating material based upon the usage of anatomical description and with the help of descriptive and analytical processes therefrom, one can arrive at a description of the essential characteristics of dance.
    I could not find any such analysis in the material made available to me. As such, this can be seen as an attempt at describing such material in a substantial way. The future of dance analysis could possibly be considered in such a way.

2. What is dance?

It is difficult to clearly define 'dance', whether based upon individual or cultural opinions. From *'movement'*, such as the flight of insects, or the 'Dance of the Bees' to *'rhythmic'*, such as the 'Dance of Stars', to the common attitude, in German "dance", in Hopi, "work" and Ewe "to make the sun turn" (Faik-Nzuij, 1993, 18).

The field of semantics varies intra and inter-linguistically, based upon a fundamentally intrapersonal and culturally-specific, implicit/explicit appreciation of dance.

The Viennese Zoologist, Karl von Frisch came to the conclusion that bees communicate in a language which manifests itself as 'dance' (von Frisch, 1965). Dance can thus be related to a type of choreographically-structured use of space, such as evidenced by the direction, focus, speed and quality of movement of the beating of the wings and the rear-end of the bee. Along with this, information is transmitted via the olfactory and acoustic channels. Human dance is creative; that of the bee, an inborn behavioural system.

Judgement of the quality, speed, dynamic of movement and stature of a dancer are inherently 'standardised' within the culture of dance. Compared to 'local' dance styles such as modern, ballet or disco dancing, the speed of the South Korean shaman dance, for example, would be judged as being too slow. The same goes for 'minimalist' dances, such as the traditional Japanese Dance, which is said to be boring and uninteresting. They do not conform to local 'tastes'.

Furthermore, students who want to study classical ballet, have to epitomise the standardised 'norm'. Both height and shape are standardised, meaning that ballet dancers are all roughly of the same size. This aesthetic can become culturally imported, hence the dancers of the Ghana Dance Group epitomize the 'slim' dancer of the West in stark contrast to their local body aesthetic: there, a beautiful woman is "round" (Yartey, 1992), or in our sense of the word, fat (Nketia, 1965, 2). The group travels overseas a great deal and has obviously adapted itself to the western idea of 'normal'.

Etymologically speaking it is not easy to determine the word dance. Kluge (1963) proposed that the word is borrowed from the French word *'danse'*; and possibly from Latin, Medieval Latin *danetzare* – "amusing oneself on a threshing floor"– or old Franconian *dansòn* – "to pull, stretch". According to Grimm, other terms were used, e.g. "gothic *laiks*, old German *salzon*, or old Saxon German *saltian*", which is derived from Latin *saltare* – "to jump, skip".

Generically, boundaries lie between mime and dramatic theatre. Brockhaus describes it as "rhythmical body movement set mostly to music" (Brockhaus, 1973, 18). Brockhaus distinguishes between 'pictureless' dance (rhythmic-dynamic) and 'representational' dance (informs, announces, imitates). The latter is not bound by rhythm and borders on mime. The boundary between generic dance and mime is similarly obscure.

Dance is universal as historically witnessed through illustration and description. The degree to which it is widespread is, however, great. Many writers have unsuccessfully tried to answer the questions, 'what is dance' and 'why people dance'. On top of that, the question is proposed in today's modern western world where dancing has lost much of its everyday meaning. One can talk of a 'dance boom' (Hörmann, 1991, 144) in discos, dance schools and in adult education but not in the same context of understanding integration within the daily life of West Africa.

> "They never miss an opportunity to dance in Africa" (Groß, 1993, 156);
> "dance is central to the life of Africans." (Bame, 1991, 7)

Here, we do not turn to our own traditional forms of dance, rather to Latin American, African, Indian, North American Indian and other cultures of dance.

The very need to pose the question also shows that as a means of natural expression in an affective and cognitive sense, dance is no longer considered a form of bodily behaviour within certain expressions and functions, rather as something "special", incomprehensible, bound with an aura of mystery (Baaren, 1964, 7).

Many attempts exist to define dance in generic terms or as a single phenomenon. They are mutually exclusive. I would like to quote and comment upon certain information concerning dance, as contained within.

> "A dance is a perception like all other works of art, which express the nature of human emotion" [...] "dance is regarded as a manifestation of strength, a dynamic work of art." (Langer, 1957, 96)

> "Dance is nothing other than Art; spiritual affairs and processes expressed through corporal rhythmic motion." (Schikowski, 1926, 9)

> "The apotheosis of movement, the highest form of gesture, the triumph of rhythm over paralysis." (Baaren, 1964, 7)

"Dance is the triumph of the body and its expressive potential." (Calendoli, 1981, 8)

"a reasonable means of inter-human communication, when language is no longer sufficient." (Schmidt, 1984, 20)

"Dance is the living language, spoken by humans and substantiating human life." (Wigman, 1963, 10)

"Dance, like speech, philosophy, painting or music, is a form of expression given to man" (Wigman, 1933, 15).

"[…] playing, an outlet for inner tensions, resulting in free, imaginative movement" (Acken, 1929, 67).

"An outward expression of that which moves humans on the inside." (Baaren, 1964, 8)

"Depending upon cultural values and attitudes the widespread phenomenon of dance proffers diverse meanings. For many ethnic groups it is very closely associated with sacred and secular acts which demonstrate the high point of societal living; dance is an integrated bedrock of the culture at large." (Weidig, 1984, 6)

"associated with one of the oldest forms of human pleasure." (Böhme, 1980, 1)

"Of all the art forms observed by man, dance is the most fundamental." (von Boehn, 1925, 7)

"Dance is a transient mode of expression, performed in a given form and style by the human body moving in space. Dance occurs through purposefully selected and controlled rhythmic movements; the resulting phenomenon is recognized as dance both by the performer and the observing members of a given group." (Kealiinohomoku, 1980, 6)

From the various extracts given above, it seems that there is a real need to arrive at some kind of definition of dance. Resulting attempts at a definition are very varied and are open to personal interpretation.

After studying the quotes, the following viewpoints appear to be the most far-reaching ones:
1. Dance is a means of expressing feelings. Dancing is an affected action. (Langer, 1959; Schikowski, 1926; Baaren, 1964; Böhme, 1980)
    One could describe this approach as psychologically motivated. (Hubert, 1992, 41ff.)

2. Dance is an art form; such as the goal in the deliberation of art theory. (Langer, 1957; Boehn, 1925; Sulzer, 1787)
3. A means of expression and communication which brings together concepts of psychology and the science of communication (Schmidt, 1984; Wigman, 1933; Wigman, 1963; Kealiinohomoku, 1980).
4. Heroising, mystifying and deifying of dance (Baaren, 1964; Calendoli, 1981).

Every description can be countered however, and deemed to be insufficient. To elevate all dance to an art form is not, in my opinion, meaningful. Firstly, because one cannot define "What is Art?" and secondly, because it seems to be such a eurocentric thing to do. Just because we define dance in terms of 'art on stage' it does not mean that other cultures have to do so as well. Dance is also used within the framework of religious ceremony and in a secular and official capacity.

Dance not only expresses feelings but also real events, such as in the mime-like 'dance stories' of the Wolof in Senegal.

Using conventional gesture and mime, the most well-known dance-narratives are to be found in India. "Dancing, as understood in India, is essentially what it was for the Greeks. Neither mere spectacle, exercise nor entertainment but rather 'the representation, by means of gestures, of things told'; a representation, that is to say, of 'myths'; the stories of gods and heroes." (LaMeri, 1941, vii)

As a means of expression and communication it is sensible to use dance, given its potential for expressing feelings and stories. To mystify and deify dance is a way of countering science, a way of illuminating perceived mysteries.

Summing up, to define the "use" of dance is a bottomless barrel. According to Peter Brinson: "It is not possible to define dance [...]" (Brinson, 1982, 8)

For the moment, the following holds true: dancing is a special form of corporal "doing", a universal, and yet culturally-specific expression, and a predominantly social act.

From the previous quotes governing characteristics of dance we can ascertain that it is:
- "active (physical) power" (Langer, 1957, 97)
- "rhythmical movement of the body" (Schikowski, 1926, 15)
- "movement [...] gestures" (Baaren, 1946, 25)
- "free, imaginative movement" (Acken, 1929, 65)

– "human body moving in space [...] rhythmic movement" (Kealiinohomo-ku, 1980, 235).

It is inherently linked to <u>motion and rhythm,</u> a function like space, time and gravity. It is <u>corporal motion through time and space</u>.

If one puts together the general, phenomenal and functional properties of dance and compares them to the spoken word one notices certain similarities which can be classified as:

		dance	spoken language
general	universal vs. culturally specific	+	+
	socially learned technique	(+)	+
phenomenal	body movement	+	(+)
functional	affected expression	+	+
	communicative	+	+
	narrative	(+)	+
	ritual	+	(+)
	aesthetic	+	(+)

Both dance and spoken language are universal means of expression depending upon the specific cultural background.

Spoken language and dance both have in common that they manifest themselves through movement; spoken language using visible and non-visible movement via articulation and dance via movement of the (entire) body. The main difference is that the body movement in dance <u>represents</u> the signal for the recipient, in spoken language, however, body movement only helps to <u>produce</u> the acoustic signal. Both ways use partly arbitrary, self-repeating and structured sequences of movement.

Spoken language and (to some extent) dance are socially-learned communication techniques. Dance is partially learnt in much the same way as our first words; through imitation.

This no longer applies to our cultural-circles, as dance is no longer a major part of our daily lives and therefore, unlike in Africa, does not fulfil any of the functions which it does in their day-to-day 'culture'.

Spoken language and, to some extent, dance perform a communicative function. Only language is a communication system in every sense. (Heike, 1960, 171)

Dance itself has a communicative function so long as the task to convey information through conventionalised gesture is fulfilled.

On the one hand, information concerning the psychological disposition (Trubetzkoy, 1939; Hammarström, 1966) of a speaker or dancer can be conveyed through language and dance, whilst, on the other hand, certain emotions can be consciously expressed in vocal or dance-like ways.

Both language (limited) and dance are aesthetic forms of expression and are of significant importance in ritual ceremonies, especially in African dance.

3. Dance and science

Different scientific disciplines such as the social sciences, ethnology, psychology and sport science have looked at dance as an object of research. Yet there is no standardised terminology relating to the subject. An outline of the different scientific approaches will be given below.

3.1 Ethnology

Non-European cultures of dance were and still are mostly studied from an ethnological point of view. In the process, the 'situation-functional' approach comes to the fore. The situational context and social function of dance will be both described and explained. An overview of the various elements of dance is detailed below (Harper, 1968).

1. Location: it can be the village square, a clearing, a stage or a sacred place.
2. Time: can be a time of day or a seasonal event such as the beginning of the rainy season.
3. Duration: it will be related to how long the dancers dance or the start and finishing times as long as that is of relevance. Details of duration correspond to a wider time span during which the dance may or must be performed. Amongst the Lugbara, for example, a dance may last for several years depending on rank and standing of the deceased. This does not mean that a dance lasts for years, rather that it should be danced if relatives or friends visit the village over the agreed period of time (Middleton, 1985).

The following details relate to the performance:
1. <u>Musical accompaniment</u>: the instruments, their formation and significance, and any vocal or textual accompaniment will be described, if made available.
2. <u>Costumes, masks and body-painting</u>: particularly relating to materials used, colours and their significance. A mask can be made from various materials to represent other 'powers'. 'Mask', in the sense of body-painting, can be partial or full-bodied. Any inherent significance will be explained.
3. <u>Dancers and musicians</u>: will be detailed with particular attention to age, gender and social status.
4. <u>The audience</u>: will also be detailed relating to age, gender, status and their way of participating.

5. <u>Aspects of choreography</u>: the spatial position, direction of movement and position of the dancer will be explained and analysed with reference to symbols and function.

Dance itself will be presented in a societal, political, religious and religious-philosophical context. A short summary will describe and explain all aspects of a particular 'event'. It should be noted, however, that the elements of a dance, here given as movement, duration, quality of movement and meaning of the sequences will not be considered.

Exemplary works of new ethnological research include those of Judith Lynn Hanna and Joanne Wheeler Kealiinohomoku. These works stand out from the mass of opinion as they do not conform to the above categorisation which tends to delineate between ballet (or modern dance) and all other ethnological forms of dance, be it folk, ethnic or primitive in form.
Both authors see dance as being of a common human activity.

Kealiinohomoku demonstrates that ballet is also a form of ethnic dance (Kealiinohomoku, 1980, 545). "It is good anthropology to think of ballet as a form of ethnic dance. Currently, that idea is unacceptable to most western scholars." (Kealiinohomoku, 1980, 533)
She regards ballet from an ethnological point of view, and looks at location, duration and type of performance, as well as the dancers and their costumes, the musical accompaniment, scenery and the substance of the piece.
The following is a précis of one of Hanna's many works, her latest, 'To Dance is Human'. Her point of view is based upon the following definition: "Dance is a conceptual, natural language with intrinsic and extrinsic meanings, a system of physical movements, and interrelated rules guiding performance in different social situations. Dance is human thought and behaviour performed by the human body and for human purposes." (Hanna, 1979, 5)
On the one hand, her "definition" is orientated towards communication theory; on the other hand, it is also sociological. Her viewpoint is not compatible with the concept of "natural language", in the sense of the word "meaning" (e. g. the meaning of gesture or dance in a specific context). Dance is valued as an autarkic phenomenon and, at the same time, as "a part of the web of human existence" (Hanna, 1979, 5). It should be examined from various academic viewpoints.
From a communications point of view, dance is an expressive form of thought, feeling and movement, a reflection of the individual or the society. Hanna subdivides ethnology as:

1. ethnological and cultural anthropology,
2. linguistic anthropology and sociolinguistics, "the ethnography of speaking" (Hanna, 1979, 7),
3. physical anthropology and
4. archaeology.

Ethnological research tries to contextualise dance within the social structure of a society. The central question is whether dance and performance reflect social structures (Hanna, 1979, 6ff.). From a cultural-anthropological viewpoint, one tries to analyse dance "patterns", in order to draw conclusions concerning community models. "The goal is to comprehend those reflecting, refracting, or innovating mechanisms of dance, that provide orientations to the realities of a group and to the ways these realities are to be conceived, felt and acted upon." (Hanna, 1979, 6)

Ethno-linguistic viewpoints which touch on Chomsky's theory make it their job to present rules of connection between shallow and deep structures of dance via rules of transformation. From a sociological point of view, dance is judged to be a system of movement, meaning and rules. The focus here is the relationship between dancer, choreographer and audience. To the physical anthropologist the focus is on studying the physical-biological: "The differences between human and dance phenomena and other similar animal patterns and [...] social relations of individuals." (Hanna, 1979, 7)

Archaeological examination is both anthropological and ethnological, whereby the data being examined includes material of a historical and pictorial nature.

Hanna succeeds in bringing the subject of dance as academic research to the fore. In my opinion, however, she provides too great a mixture of terminologies from various sciences, whereupon one is left with the impression that it interferes with the very subject of research. The use of this terminology is sometimes rather ambiguous. In the chapter "Dance Movement and the Communication of Socio-cultural Patterns", technical terms such as "social taxonomies", "design features of languages versus design features of dance" and "minimal units" are used without clarifying them in relation to speech or dance.

She also uses concepts such as 'deep and shallow structures' whilst not making it clear how they conform to transformational generative grammar. Dance research should provide a "set of rules" relating to "deep and shallow" dance structures, "which describe how the realm of movement is related to the realm of meaning." (Hanna, 1979, 7)

There is no doubt that, within certain parameters, parallels between speech and body-language exist (of which dance is one form) which should be further clarified, above all else from the point of view of the communication function.

Just how far we should go back to linguistic theory, varies from case to case.

3.2 The psychological approach

The most important exponents of Dance Psychology are L. Espenak, M. Peter-Bolaender, F. Reichelt und T. Schopp. Most exponents align themselves with dance therapy. Their concepts are based on C.G. Jung, A. Lowen, and A. Adler's theories of psychology or the gestalt-based therapy of Perls. To establish humans as psycho/physiological entities, 'free dance' is utilised as a prophylactic or therapeutic step, to help humans maintain their psycho–physiological balance.

Hörmann (1991) divides Dance Psychology into:
1. "What we can learn from psychological, dance-inherent 'events' and their effects on composition, improvisation and interpretation."
   Psychological disposition leads to individual and dance-like, improvisational movement. The dance event is dismantled and analysed in its elements. The elements being the type and form of movement, their structure, their choreography, relation to space and speed of motion. We recognise many ways of looking at dance, analysing such factors as space, time and flow. Based upon this analysis, conclusions of psychological disposition will be made and the motivating force behind dance eventually explained.

> **psychological disposition** ------------- **dance event**

2. "The lessons learnt from dance-related events and their utilization"
   What happens when dancing solo or with someone, what are the effects, consequences and what psychological events are evoked?

> **dance event** ----------- **psychological effects**

One can conclude from both of the above, that in terms of its 'production', dance is governed by emotion. This view is somewhat limited, as dance is also a thoroughly intellectual activity, as evidenced in 'language-based' displays such as the "Bharatanatyam' dance of southern India.

3.3 Historical perspectives

There are a multitude of historical treatises on dance, from the overall picture to works illuminating certain epochs, the oldest being by Lucian. It concerns a fictitious dialogue (in poetic form) between Lycinus and Kraton and is about the "Art of Dancing" in Greece at that time. It antithetically looks at the pros and cons of dance, which according to Lycinus was a 'God-given talent'. Lycinus, on the side of 'pro', reflected dance of its time. He details ritual and war dances from Phrygia, on Crete and in Thessaloniki. He refers to non-Greek dance, such as from India, Ethiopia, Egypt and from the Romans, quoting from literary sources such as Homer, Hesiod and Socrates. From various references and comments, one gathers that dances were accompanied by music and song. Commentary of movement has not been considered in any sense. The writer notes that, "The dancer had to be skilled in the art of movement, be born soft and strong, supple and sinewy so that his limbs could do all manner of bending and then collect himself to stand as stock-still or in any manner required for his role." (Lukian, 1922, 97)

Nitschke gives us a vision of dance in the Middle Ages and during the Renaissance. Various historical texts and illustrations of the time point to the existence of dance amongst the aristocracy. We also know that apart from solo and ensemble dance, dancing in pairs was also common. The author also refers to elements of choreography in dance, as "all dances seemed to display a variety of ornament-like patterns." (Nitschke, 1987, 72) Regarding the presented extracts, this decoding of pictorial material was clearly flawed in its interpretation. A diagonal was thus described as a line, and he overlooks certain illustrated movements which clearly contain elements of technical dance. Furthermore, he uses illustrations dating from the 9th century, which clearly relate to biblical texts, as evidence of dance in the Middle Ages. Given the way people are presented, their clothing, their headwear and the architecture, which is clearly from the Middle Ages, one could draw the wrong conclusion, namely, that the illustrated 'dancers' truly represent an accurate portrayal of that time.

Boehn (1925), Hagemann (1919), W. Ridgeway (1925), Sachs (1937) und Schikowski (1926) offer both historical and culture-historical perspectives.

Boehn and Schikowski both dedicate a chapter of their works to indigenous peoples, that is to say non-European cultures, from North American Indian to Chinese to African tribal dance. They dedicate other parts of their works to European dance in its historical form. Hagemann and Ridgeway unveil detailed insight into non-European dance culture. The main focus is on its origin and the development of dance.

Klein refers to dance in cave paintings from the Palaeolithic era and the frescos of Cabal Huyuk in Turkey (Klein, 1994, 17ff.). Lange also comments on historical illustrations which demonstrate the historical existence of dance (Lange, 1975). These works do not disclose, however, which features the authors accept as 'indicative' of the fact that the illustrations are representative of sequences of dance-like movement.

3.4 Semiotic, linguistic and phenomenological approaches

In her study, Ness (1987) researched the symbolic meaning of several parts of the Sinulog, a religious dance from the Philippines, based on the Child Jesus.

Analysis of movement is part of the overall analysis of the extensive symbolism of the dance. The way of moving expresses the culturally-inherent notion of terms such as movement (linok), openness (kinasingkasing) and victim (halad). The dance is seen as a collective symbolic act. She establishes: the monadic aspects of the symbolic process; dancing as in the form of bodily movement; the didactic aspect, meaning the effect on the 'performance space'; the triadic aspect, being the presentation of particular elements of the performance and their relationship to features of the cultural framework.

Ikegami undertakes an analysis of hand gesturing in classical Indian dance using stratificational grammar. (There have been lexicons describing hand, foot and head gestures for a long time, the first illustrated version dating back to approximately 450–100 B.C.) In classical Indian dance, finger, hand, arm, leg and foot positions function as distinctive entities. 'Karana' or "single posture" is a complex position of hand gestures (Ikegami, 1971, 375), torso, head and legs.

There are six 'sthanaka' (torso and head positions), 32 'caris' (leg and foot positions) and 27 'nritta hastas' (hand gestures). A combination of two 'karanas' makes one completed action. With use of analysis, the author impeccably shows individual hand gestures, of both hands, and clearly demonstrates that a full description of the system of hand gestures is possible.

"That a communication system is describable in terms of strata means that it has a certain number of sets of basic elements that are related to each other hierarchically in such a way that members of one set can be said to be 'realizations' of those of a second set, and those of the second set realizations of those of a third set, and so on." (Ikegami, 1971, 375)

Hubert's (1992) phenomenological study is based on the principle of the nature of dance being socio-theoretical. He researches dance in the context of its "socio-human" activity. Categories of activity are "action, content and movement" (Hubert, 1992, 18f.). The methodological guideline ranges from abstract to concrete, with the following constituents:

1. The phenomenon 'dance' as part of daily life exists in two forms:
   a) as a tangible event (dance event)
   b) in literature concerning dance and dancing.
   Thus both are a tangible and a linguistic manifestation.
2. Given the above, the analytical process leads us to the very origins of dance, the "cell-form"; the constituent parts of the subject. It is a fundamentally genetic and theoretical thing, not entirely coincidental and specific in form. The "cell-form" is the result of the scientific analysis of research.
3. Analysing the individual parts leads one to construct a theoretically understandable picture and "thus to a definitive and clarified subject." The ensuing 'definitive thought' is a "structured, logically-dialectic interrelation of terminology, category, argument and statement of law" (Nketia, 1979, 261ff.).

In conclusion: the breaking down of the abstract into its separate parts gives us the "cell-form" and leads to 'definitive thought', through presentation and discussion of the analysis.

3.5 African dance as a subject of musicology and ethnology

It is mostly musicologists and ethnologists who have examined African dance. Scientific discipline itself assesses the degree to which a subject is to be scrutinised.

No standardised terminology exists relating to this subject of research.

Noteworthy musicologists are Dauer (1969, 15), Günther (1963; 1968; 1969) and Nketia (1979) from Ghana. Rather than mere musicology, Nketia's work clearly stems from his own practical experience and will therefore be well-drawn upon and elucidated. He refers to the conversion of rhythmic structure into bodily gesture. He formulates certain rules relating to the relationship and combination of music with dance.

Referring to the Akan-Dances, 'adowa' and 'sikyi', Nketia describes the prevailing rules:
- "Firstly, the recognition and relevant articulation of the controlling beat. The basic steps separate the time-measure, as given by a bell, into two or multiples thereof." (Nketia, 1979, 168)
- "Secondly, movement of the various parts of the body, hands and torso are coordinated with steps as dictated by the metre."
- "Thirdly, the speed of movement. Speed can be expressed using rhythm, note length or a drumroll."
- "The fourth rule deals with articulation of irregular rhythms and the orientation of the dancer to them."
- "Phrasing is the fifth rule. As a drummer can play clear disjointed patterns, each introduced pattern can be repeated. This allows the dancer to structure his movement with phrases, pauses and concluding gestures with his legs, hands, head etc." (Nketia, 1979, 261f.)

Rules 2 and 5 are reminiscent of what Günther, in support of the term 'Polyrhythm in music' describes as Polycentric technique. "Polycentricity is the basis of dance technique", underlines the principle of Polycentricity (Günther, 1969, 15).

It means that different axes of bodily movement move independently of each other (cervical, vertebrae, thoracic vertebrae, lumbar, pelvis, arms, hands and legs). Furthermore, rules 1 and 5 acknowledge the 'Principle of Isolation', which states that centres of motion can be "moved in isolation from one another given divergent rhythmic phrasing." (Groß, 1993, 168) Günther explains about corporal, motional, movement and musical characteristics of Afro-American Dance. He uses North American jazz dance terminology which evolved out of dance studios and the music itself. Polycentricity, isolation and polyrhythm are fundamental to dance. One can isolate the various axes of movement in the body.

In contrast to ballet, where torso, pelvis, hand and arm present unity of movement at any one time, in African dance there are different "upper and lower-body pivot-points" (Günther, 1969, 16). They can be independently 'isolated' and moved. The dance form is 'inflected' (Günther, 1969, 23), which means that knees are bent and the upper body diagonally inclined forwards. In my opinion Günther wrongly interprets this aspect of African dance, with reference to Polycentricity (Günther, 1969, 1). "Polycentricity should infer that neither the dancer nor his body experience 'unity', rather that he 'self-destructs' his body, dissolves into it, tears it apart. The result is that of religiously-experienced ecstasy. The audience cannot be fully aware of the dancer's physical experience. 'Feeling by doing', in a subjective sense, here means harmony rather than discord. Further training would result in ever more 'fluid movement'. One should judge dancers by their elegance and their fluidity of motion rather than discord.

In my opinion Günther confuses dance and euphoria. It has been observed that euphoria can be brought on through movement, in Tigare (Ghana), for example, likewise the Dervish dance of the Sufi or Shamanic trance-dancing. The prescribed and structured patterns of dance can disintegrate into unstructured 'motor activity'. This condition is clearly euphoric. A state of euphoria has still not been clearly explained, or if it is indeed the movement, the music or the drugs which bring it about.

To this day, Günther's is the one work which tries to classify African dance using movement-theory. Dauer (1967) provisionally proposed a structure for regional dance styles from western Sudan, Sahara, the West African coast, the Central African Bantu and Southern Bantu. He exploits the notion of pivot points to enable an organisation of the characteristics of dance.

High jumping characterises east African and Saharan dance. In central Africa, movement is characterised by the maximum use of the pelvis. Alongside this, minimalist, upper-body movements using minimal space. On the West African coast, one finds "multiplication technique" through the use of leg and foot gesturing. The dancer enhances the use of the off-beats through steps and jumps. The dancer converts 'rhythmic-pattern' into 'motion-pattern' to visually enhance the musical structure. This characteristic is thus both motion and music related. Using these characteristics is not the only way, however, of defining regions of dance.

The Lolo, Fume-fume and Dabila dances of the Ga in Ghana use jumping with many minimalist movements, as with various dances of the Susu in Guinea. There is also a difference between genders. Dances, which would normally have been danced by women, are more 'minimalistic' in contrast to the acrobatic, spatial jumping of men. Within certain dances of the Wolof, Ga and Susu, gender restrictions do not seem to apply anymore. The Saba of the Wolof used to only be danced by women. It is full of gentle and glowing 'minimalistic' movement. Formerly, men who danced the Saba would have been identified as gay or feminine.

From an ethnological standpoint, there is greater discourse over certain dances of individual peoples. A description of these works is made within the context of the religions and social networks in which dance is embedded, through which it is expressed and any pertinent philosophical background is explained.

Considering the criteria such as noted below, very little mention has been made of the motion, choreography, content or meaning of movement. It may be that because movement is ephemeral by nature, it is more difficult to comprehend. It is not possible to illustrate 'movement' without having the means to 'segmentalise' dance sequences. Faced with a flurry of movement, the untrained eye is neither able to understand nor see any structure in it, let alone describe it.

4. The Ewe

The Ewe-speaking people live in the region that is in southeastern Ghana and southern Togo. They are bordered to the east by the Fon people and to the West by the Adangme, Ga and Akan. Geomorphologically, it is mountainous to the north and then descends via open plains, to the southern coast. Important towns in the area are Keta and Denu in Ghana and Anexo and Lomé (the capital) in Togo. All four towns are coastal and of economic importance. The fishing and salt-production industries are well represented here.

The Ewe live in two politically and governmentally-contrasting states. English is the official language of Ghana, in Togo it is French. As such, the Ewe are multi-lingual. Made up of groups such as the Anlo, Sorie, Be and Ge, the total population numbers more than one million.

The geographical roots of the Ewe and their ethno-genetic group are unclear. They migrated out of Ketu, Benin. Ketu demonstrates political unity and grew from one of the more major settlements and migrants from the surrounding area. It dates from the 12th or 13th centuries (Asamoa, 1971, 26). Conflict within the Yoruba area around Ketu led the Ewe to resettle in the southern region, of what is known as Togo nowadays. From the middle of the 17th century onwards, the Ewe emigrated from there back to the regions mentioned above.

Further conflict over fishing and salt-production rights during the slavery period in pre-colonial Africa led to war on more than one occasion. This led to factions and alliances with non-Ewe groups. Segregation was not permanent, however, and trade relations were ongoing. The Ewe were politically and officially separated during the period of enforcement of the colonially-imposed frontiers and have remained so, even given 20th century attempts at re-unification.

5. The Ewe language

Ewe belongs to the Niger-Congo family of languages, subgroup 'Kwa'. "It is sometimes not possible to arrive at a consensus of meaning between some of the many dialects of Ewe." (Heine, 1968, 161)

The first to document the language were the Bremen Missionaries, of whom Westermann was the first to record aspects of grammar. The influence of the Ewe has grown since the documentation of their language.

As with many West African languages, Ewe is a tone language. This means that pitch and pitch changes have great influence on meaning. "A tone language may be defined as a language having lexically significant, contrastive, but relative pitch on each syllable." (Pike, 1957, 3)

The drum is not only a rhythmic but also a melodic instrument (Chernoff, 1994, 99). Spoken language is 'translated' into drum-language by the musician. Using his technique he can introduce characteristics of quantity and pitch into his drumming.

"Drum signaling [...] may be said to render the tonal and length-factors of speech accurately enough. It reflects quite faithfully the essential structural pattern of the language, including some of the more intricate details of the constitution of the 'mora' or syllable." (Herzog, 1945, 233)

In his study, Herzog (1945) identifies that drum language is a 'conventionalised code'. In his work, John Miller Chernoff refers to Ewe drummers who have thus communicated over a long period of time. In his article about drum language as a system of communication, Herzog states: "The African systems are the most elaborate and often serve for conversation." (Herzog, 1945, 217)

6. Religion in Ewe Society

One comes across several religions, both indigenous and 'imported'. Scriptures, services and the element of participation vary and both women and men serve in an official capacity. It is mainly in the older religions of the Ewe that one comes across references to dance.

The following will detail the stigmatising of dance by the Christian missionaries and discuss the consequences. There are two ways in which the early work of the missionaries brought about the demise of dance:

a) Missionaries were the original source of knowledge and thus provided a vantage point from which to view research in Africa, and

b) their activities, such as the banning of traditional culture (here meant as historical dance), has made such research rather obscure nowadays.

The Basel and Bremen (North German society of Missionaries) missions undertook the 'missionising' of the Ewe. Lorenz Wolf began the task of building the inland mission in 1847, following an invitation from King Kwadwo II. Others followed with their wives (Spieth, 1911, 5ff.). Various illnesses and mortalities lead to missionaries moving to the coast. In 1853 the base remained Keta, although mortalities continued to occur given acclimatisation problems. In the first 50 years, of a total of 157 men and women, 64 people died and 56 returned home.

Stations in Waya and Wegbe were destroyed during the Ashanti-Ewe war of 1869 and others had to be evacuated. The Bremen Mission took up its work five years later after the English victory over the Ashanti in Kumasi.

The 'Zanzibar Contract' established colonial borders in 1980. Togo became a German colony, whereby the Bremen Mission intensified its work, particularly in schooling, with control over 62 schools in the German sector and 32 in the British sector.

A further consequence of acclimatisation problems was the schooling of Ewe missionaries in Germany. The privilege of catechist training leading to priesthood (Osofo) was given to selected individuals with leadership qualities and ten years of experience of missionary work.

Togo was divided between France and England and the influence of the missions reduced as the administration separated schools from the church's sphere of influence (Beyreuther, 1978).

Why was dance deemed so disreputable? Set against the backdrop of the traditions of the institutionalised church, one realises why the missionaries could not appreciate its relevance and why this attitude prevails as evidenced by a lack of interest in researching the subject.

One can understand the impossibility of appreciating the unboundedness of dance in Africa when looking at our own traditional heritage.

Christian Europe 'danced', of course, but within the confines of 1700 years of Christianity; its physicality was crushed by morality. Dance embodied frivolity and reprehensibility even for those of rational thinking.

Traditionally rigid and moralistic views, in the case of the implicit and explicit judgement of the 'importance' assigned to the body and to dance, can be intellectually challenged and eventually eradicated, but may by no means give rise to a feeling of behavioural change.

The Bremen missionaries lived under the spiritual tradition of protestant piety. Moral, ethical and paedagogical principles stemmed from August Hermann Francke, amongst others. Hinrichs implies piety is "a socio-religious movement within itself, with worldwide, universal objectives." (Hinrichs, 1971, 1) This movement was to a certain extent against the Lutheran reforms, which had not managed to eradicate "the evil and imperfections of the world." (Hinrichs, 1971, 1)

The evolution of Mankind, in a positive sense, is accordingly the precondition of change in the world and the eradication of its political and social problems. Churches and schools undertake the job of transforming man. Education, research and the expansion of knowledge should serve to spread pious ideals. Pietism thus developed into a 'commercial' and missionary venture, for all manner of languages had to be learnt so as to facilitate the spread of (pious) Christian belief and the translation of the Bible. Linguistic exploration of the 'local language' was thus extensively pursued in the Togo missions. The fundamentals for research into 'Ewe' were laid down by the missionaries Knüsli and Schlegel. The latter derived the initial grammar, and Westermann the first dictionary of Ewe. Amongst others, Spieth translated the Bible into Ewe based upon prior linguistic research.

To a large extent and to their great credit, the work of the missionaries, in researching and textualising the spoken language, has formed the present-day basis of West African linguistic research.

In 1902 (March to December), detailed letters to his superior, Westermann describes the problems of textualising Ewe, deriving it's grammar and the editing and translation of the Bible (Westermann, 1902). The missionaries did, however, almost permanently close the door on research into 'body language' and thus dance too. One cannot posthumously judge them, however, as they were, likewise victims of what can only be termed 'physical suppression'.

As 'children of their time', the missionaries, condemned dance as being reprehensible and sinful. In their thoughts and on paper too, dance was indecent, sexualised so to speak. The act of dancing was in itself, indecent.

The pious way of living was one of extreme abstinence. Games, happiness, fun and enjoying life were 'forbidden'. This included a turning away from all sinful pleasure and a turning towards "Godliness". Godliness did not include creative or joyful expression of things playful or corporeal. Francke views the body as the servant rather than the master and as such to accept "bread, punishment and work" as its lot. He was a harsh critic of dance. In a "thorough and detailed answer to the question: what does one think of common dance?", he reveals his opinion of dance: one should distance oneself from such "common filth". Besides, dance awakens the "craving for flesh" and is, without exception, sinful.

One can surmise that:
- the creative entity, "homo ludens", was totally incomprehensible to Pietism.
  Confinement of free bodily movement for both sexes – although it affected girls and boys differently – was the ideal of a pious upbringing. One achieved this via all possible means: proclaiming bodily acts as embarrassing and shameful, physical chastisements and by implanting the idea that God punished.
- the tactile communication mechanism in intra- and interpersonal contact was closed. Physically touching, an important situational variable (Scherer, 1970, 76) in communication and in physio-psychological health was denounced as a sin.
- pious upbringing suppresses sexuality. Sexuality is functional reproduction and not recognised as a part of lust or the erotic.

The missionary mind probably equated every physical contact with the "devil's work" (sexuality) as a result of such bans. An extensive and perceptive understanding of the African 'culture of movement' was thus not possible, let alone researched. Dance was prejudged to be a demonstration of physicality, a 'craving for flesh', idleness and as such, sinful.

This must all have led to a completely false understanding of dance and ultimately to the banning of dance by the missionaries. This view of dance as the 'devil's work' was one-sided and did not reflect its value in the sense of cultural history.

This negation of dance is neither evidenced in the Bible nor in the work of Martin Luther. One can find references to dance in the Old and New Testaments. Luther apparently favoured the Shrovetide and dance (Kutter, 1958, 161). To him, dance was an adiaphora; a part of life. Dance was first denounced by his successor. Luther addressed the issue in the 'Lent Post' of 1525 (Luther, 1525).

Luther's opinion that dance itself is not a sin, 'neither being good nor bad', is also the opinion of Herod's daughter. This episode of the Bible is always pulled upon to cast aspersions on dance. It has been used by John Chrysostom to condemn dance and shows just how old the 'tradition' of condemning dance in Christianity is:

> "Where there is dance, there is the devil. God did not give us feet to dance, rather to stride ahead in harmonious unity; not to dance with camels, rather with angels. When such disorder shames the body, it does so much more than the soul." (Sudbrodt, 1995, 164)

Salome danced on the occasion of Herod's birthday. Her dance pleased him so much that, in front of his guests, he promised the young lady anything she so desired. Salome asked her mother, who answered that she should ask for the head of John the Baptist on a plate. Herod was somewhat "distressed", because he both feared and admired his righteousness, "and he listened to him." He did nonetheless not want to lose face in front of his guests: "He wanted to keep his word and the goodwill of his companions [...]". (Die Bibel, 1997, 1137, Markus)

We can glean the following: his daughter danced beautifully. Her mother advised the daughter to her own ends. It was more important for Herod to 'save face' rather than follow his conscience. Also, relating to Chrysostom, dance was mixed-up in the morbid wishes of her mother and the deeds of her father. Later interpretations of this story project their own erotic, fantastic images onto this dance. Illustrations from the period suggest its possible oriental origins, thus further eroticising its original content. The story reveals elements of sin; not that the dance itself was indeed sinful.

After Luther, Puritans and the pious alike turned their vehemence on dance. They judged it. At the outset it seems that the common folk were indeed very happy to dance at weddings and other such events otherwise they would not have had to have been scolded with such emphasis (Heyer, 1975). The question as to 'if' and 'how' Protestants are allowed to dance is an issue even up to the present day.

The general insecurity originates from, amongst other things, pietistic rejection of dance because of the fear and suppression of physicality.

The 'statutes of the Evangelical Community of the Basel Mission on the Gold Coast' in the year 1902, stated under Point 1, paragraph 31 of 'conditions for the baptising of gentiles':

> "Those who are or want to be baptised in the name of Jesus Christ, must not be associated with idol 'worship', heathen festivals, burial ceremonies, dance or the like."

Just how this paragraph impacted upon life in the community and how difficult it was for the missionaries to eradicate traditional dance culture, is set out in their correspondence. Numerous letters from missionaries and their wives refer to dancing at births, deaths and religious ceremonies. Dancing was a part of the socialisation process and was learnt through imitation. A missionary wife, Julia Fies, described a burial ceremony in Dome, at which people moved thus:

> "One after the other they came and moved in ways with appealing, rhythmical movements. Just at the moment when a young girl wanted to join in, a Mawule of similar age to us, broke away from us and took hold of the girl and held onto her until we reached them. This is not the first time that we have been allowed to witness that they are developing a feeling for 'that which is not proper'" (Archives of Bremen Mission 7, 1025, 1910).

This quote infers that, both the German missionaries and the Ewe who worked at the mission, had already rejected dance and that the Mawu had already taken action to suppress it.

The letters confirm the existence of dance and documents dances which are contemporary in form and function. In his letter of 15th October 1910, Spies refers to the 'Agbeko', which is still danced today. This and a further letter from Bürgi (Oct 1910) mention the existence of the 'Siba Saba dance' as the devil's work.

> "How very busy the wicked one is, […] his news, as witnessed in a new dance, is spreading everywhere like a forest fire, especially on the coast […] they sing dirty songs to it, so Christians should be warned against it."

The 1902 guidelines for the acceptance of gentiles into the Evangelical church community state that a person could only be admitted if they had renounced dancing and drumming. From the end of 1915 to mid-1916 missionaries wrote letters of response to Bürgi's question: "In what way can we educate our community for us to be rid of this heathen dance?" 'Heathen dance' seemed to have made a comeback with the outbreak of war. Asdasu wrote that all community members grew up on 'heathen dance' and that one should treat it with consideration rather than punishment or else people would turn away from Christianity.

Kwasi called for all teachers who showed an interest in dance to be dismissed. The theologian, Asieni, stressed that converted Christians who dance, fall back into 'heathendom'. One should continue to forbid Christians to dance. Godwin Agbodza from Santrokofi, proposed that Christians should live separately and be constantly monitored by teachers. They should be "fed on songs and prayers." If they overlook the ban they should be fined "10 Pf". He otherwise encouraged virgin Christian girls and boys, "to be treated with love."

The guidelines of the Church Missions and the 1910–1915 correspondence that ensued between Akpafu, Santrokofi, Lomé, Agu, Ho and Atakpame support assumptions made that dance:
- should be forbidden,
- was sinful,
- was viewed as being synonymous with lust and sexuality,
- was misinterpreted,
- should be, and was, prevented by various means.

Furthermore,
- the historical existence of dance was verified.
- that dance was part of socialisation and learnt through imitation.
- that at births, funerals and other official and religious functions, dance played a role.
- that the Agbekor dance existed, as it does today.

The reinstatement of dance in the Christian mass has been referred to by various authors. A plausible reason seems to me to be Uzukwu's argument of why a 10,000 year old tradition is included in the Christian Liturgy: "They look at the African myth of the body completely differently, passing it on verbally from generation to generation. For them the body is neither shameful nor an instrument of sin rather the total manifestation of the person in gesture form. Its organisational and individual development reveals the true person. In a remarkable way dance can express the many experiences and ways in which we relate to the universe." (Uzukwu, 1995, 227f.)

Also that: "The sound of the human voice and particularly that of the drum moves the body to dance, giving the group and the individual the required stimulation to consciously make it 'self-aware' in relation to others." Life moves itself rhythmically along its path to its destination (its fulfilment). The human community and every individual therein find themselves on the way to 'perfection', on the way to something else. This 'movement towards something' also a 'connection' is the most fundamental element in the social definition of 'Person' and 'community.'" (Uzukwu, 1995, 228)

To Europeans, the perceived wonder and 'naturalness' of African dance, stems from their most profoundly-rooted view that the "body is [...] neither disgraceful nor an instrument of sin".

7. Preconsiderations in Communication Theory

Saussure describes linguistic symbols as 'two-sided' (Saussure, 1967). The components are "psychological" and "something already there in the spirit."

The symbol is the connection between two components; **thought/phonetic sequence** and "articulation". The thought itself is "denotative" and articulation the "denotation".

Denotative and the denotation together make the symbol. So defined, the symbol possesses two attributes: it is both <u>arbitrary</u> and <u>linear</u>. According to Saussure there is no "inner (natural) connection" between the thought and the representative **phonetic sequence**. Symbols are in this sense arbitrary and based upon convention. "Any group 'received' means of expression is actually based upon collective habit or, similarly, on convention."

Based upon the arbitrariness of symbols, Saussure makes the point that the science of Semiology as a subject of research, is worth investigating. He poses the question as to whether, "forms of expression, based upon 'natural (therefore not coincidental) symbols' – such as mime –" should be the subject of semiology. Semiology is thus the science of spoken symbols.

Hjelmslev sees symbols – exclusively spoken ones – as being something that are "meant to be something else." (Hjelmslev, 1974, 47) The symbol is a 'bearer of meaning'. It is a way of expressing something, which has a meaning. There is an interchangeable dependency between expression and meaning. The symbol-function is only achieved by the simultaneous existence of both these constituent parts, the so-called functive-elements. "There would never be a symbol-function without the simultaneous existence of these two elements. An expression and its meaning, or a meaning and its expression would never co-exist without the 'symbol-function' being there between them."

Hjelmslev also gives precedence to spoken expression in communication matters, whether phylogenetic or ontogenetic. Language is, "in itself a passive thing, a structure 'sui generis.'"

Thus far detailed, the explanation of the nature of symbols is insufficient for this paper. To that end one must revisit certain terminology and expand upon it. In their work, Pierce and then Bense addressed this with a more comprehensive understanding.

> "A symbol represents something and will, as such, be understood by man." (Bense, 1967, 9)

"A symbol is everything that can be defined and only defined, symbolically. Every 'thing' can be defined as a symbol." (Bense, 1967,10)

To that end, the term 'symbol', only usually linked to spoken language, was enlarged to bring about an understanding of non-verbal expression, according to the theory of symbols.

According to Bense there exists a 'triadic' relation amongst 'things' aided by a designated 'object'.

	Tool / mean symbol token sign	
	Sign and Symbol	
Object		Analyst / Evaluator

Table 1 (Bense, 1967, 9)

The 'symbol carrier' can be an optical or acoustic signal. The object can either be a thing or some facts. The characteristic relates to 'commentator'/'evaluator'/'analyst'.

There is therefore an interrelationship between device and object, as well as between device, object and analyst. This states that a motion, either simple or complex, can function as a symbol if the above conditions (of the characterisation of an object) are established for an analyst.

The definition of 'symbol' as used in linguistic research is, however, not sufficient. Relating to this paper, using Pierce and Bense's wider meaning of the term symbol, I propose that:

A simple or complex motion, that is a 'device' assigned to an object (be it a subject or factual) and that is understood by the recipient, is a symbol.

One can distinguish between
a) symbolic,
b) iconic and
c) indexed/deictic symbols.

The modern 'performance experience', such as witnessed at dance festivals or normal celebrations, exhibits dance to be a coded, semiotic system. The dancers, musicians, the plot itself, the dancing and music-making are all constituent parts of the symbol system. Another system represents the costumes, hairstyles, make-up and presentation of the musicians. A further system is that of the space, properties and time of day on which the performance occurs (Fischer-Lichte, 1988). With dance now at the fore, one should look more closely at the dancer himself and his actions.

The dancer is a symbol of 'something else', meaning that, in battle, he 'plays' the soldier, rather than is one. He is a symbol for another person. Person X dances the role of Y and person Z (the audience) watches. This 'doing' of the person who is acting, the dancer, is also a sign of something else; namely acting out the role of the soldier. Acting out is not real in the sense of war, rather a portrayal thereof. On the one hand, the plot/dance is a motion-form portrayal of the music, symbols and of the musical structure. On the other hand, dance is the conversion of the talking-drum text into motion form.

Textualised motion takes the place of spoken text. It has become a symbol itself; a symbol of a symbol.

8. Comparison of verbal and non-verbal forms of communication

Spoken language is universal and, in the broadest sense, an acquired technique of interpersonal and intrapersonal communication. It is a system of conventional symbols. The symbols are arbitrary as long as they are not onomatopoeic, which are phonetically imitative. Spoken language is the result of articulatory movement, the signal requirements of a sender and a receiver. This gives us the following chain:

Sender (speaker, expedient)	signal	Receiver (listener, recipient)

Speaker and listener interact via an inventory of symbols in order to communicate. Moreover, both have their own 'system' and no two systems are alike. For communication to function, both parties must possess a sufficient number of common symbols.

Both interact using external feedback which gives some control over speech signals.

Hearing	Central Nervous System	Phonation/Articula-tion	Signal	Hearing	Central Nervous System	Phonation/Articula-tion

Spoken language possesses several functions of expression in interpersonal communication. It not only conveys our thoughts but also our declaration of emotion and fulfils many social functions.

Interpersonal communication utilises all channels of communication whether consciously or subconsciously. These include gesture (hand and arm motion), facial expression, eye-movement and focus, proximity, tactility and posture. The interlocutor bases his reactions upon signals received. Communication systems of non-acoustic channels also exist but have been comparatively little researched.

Tactile, olfactory and heat perception channels

It is only during the last 30 years that form and function of the above channels have been looked at. Although not absolutely relevant to this work, they will be briefly considered.

The function of the three channels (tactile, olfactory and thermal), thus far researched:
- the psychological disposition to recognition, whereby the signal is not consciously controlled (olfactory/thermal),
- the physiological disposition and intention, whether conscious or not, to make something known (tactile): for example, by touching someone's arm when expressing sympathy.
- gaining spatial awareness, whereby the signal sender is not human.

Frank (1957) offered an oversight into the meaning of tactile communication and its intercultural differences. Jourard (1966) researched tactile behaviour in communication terms.

Hall (1966) referred to the significance of the skin not only in a spatial sense, but also in the assessment of psychological temperament. He cited a study by Hall and Brodey into the spatial awareness of blind people using their perception of thermal fluctuations in a room. "Hence we had reason to believe that it was more than the heightened sense of hearing that enabled this group to successfully [...], repeated instances were reported in which the radiant heat of objects was not only detected but had been used as an aid in navigation. A brick wall on the north side of a given street was identified as a landmark to the blind because it radiated heat over the total width of the sidewalk." (Hall, 1966, 55)

The importance of thermal fluctuations given an awareness of psychological constitution is mentioned, however only backed-up by personal observation and based upon reflection.

8.1 The visual channel

Spoken language is audible but also partly visual. For example, one can 'see' articulation of the lips (Fuster-Duran, 1966). Non-verbally, the *entire* body is a potential signal sender, not just sequentially (as in the case of verbal speech) but also simultaneously. There is also the use of body language, a further system of socially-learnt conventions. Here too, sender and receiver have to possess a similar inventory of symbolic understanding. The result is that of 'motion' based upon a visually perceived and further "apperceived" signal. The chain of communication preferred by Heike (1975):

Sender (expedient)	**Optic signal**	Receiver (Recipient)

Laban (1988) coined the term 'work-related movement' to delimit 'dance-movement' as an artistic means of expression. 'Work-related movement' implies that movement can also be a set of work-like actions, such as writing, violin playing or walking. It does not have to convey a meaning.

Birdwhistell originated the term 'kinetics' for body language (Birdwhistell, 1970). 'Body language is inadequate for it conveys the idea of phonated language, rather than the metaphorical use of the word. Kinaesthetics refers to the systematic use of gesture, facial expression and posture as part of inter-personal (spoken) communication. He limited the term to the use of gesture supporting the spoken language. The term conveys the general opinion over non-verbal communication nowadays, of which gesture and facial expression are but two components. Ekman and Friesen enlarge the subject of Kinaesthetics research and distinguish **four** principal categories:

1) Symbolic   Nonverbal, quasi-spoken, such as gestures of greeting

2) Illustratory   Movements relating to spoken expression which 'illustrate' the word(s)

3) Regulatory   Actions which have a controlling influence in the act of speaking

4) Adaptive   Signs, fundamentally characterising bodily functions such as eye-lid movement

Argyle distinguished between conversions and subconscious communication, although sender and receiver possess varying degrees of conscious-awareness.

	Sender	Receiver	
(1)	conscious	conscious	gestures such as pointing with a finger
(2)	mostly subconscious	mostly conscious	most non-verbal communication
(3)	subconscious	subconscious, but with effect	pupil enlargement, exchange of glances
(4)	conscious	subconscious	the sender is used to adapting to spatial relationships
(5)	subconscious	conscious	receiver is used to interpreting body posture

Table 2 (Argyle, 1992, 17)

The aforementioned subdivision of the subconscious and conscious is, however, meaningless for the following reasons:

a) re (1): By "conscious", the author means that convention is made out of non-verbal expression and functions as a spoken-linguistic expression. Pointing the finger is a deictic sign. Sender and receiver consciously understand the meaning of this non-verbal expression.
b) re (2): For the receiver to consciously understand non-verbal expression, one must assume that basic understanding already exists between the two. Here, the author means 'subconscious', in a), a way which relates to the meaning of the sign. 'Conscious', as used in a) and b) is not consistent.
c) re (4) and (5): Here too, the mixing-up of 'consciousness of deed' and 'consciousness of meaning' as non-verbal signs. If the receiver understands some form of body language that the sender himself is not conscious of, then some kind of code convention already exists.

It seems more sensible to speak of the deictic expression of conventionalised body-language, or pertinent and meaningful motion, as opposed to 'reflexes' which are revealed as motion.

Summary

Provisionally listed functions of non-verbal, motional behaviour:
1. <u>Functional motion:</u>
   'Work-related' movement including all aspects of locomotion.

2. <u>Expression of feeling through motion:</u>
   Partially conventionalised but not meaningful in a spoken sense, e. g. the shameful lowering of eyes. There is no 'meaning' in this action, as compared to a shrug when asked: "What time is it?" Here, the shrug clearly means: "I don't know."

3. <u>Motion as an expression of meaning with a quasi-spoken language function:</u>
   Conventionalised, meaningful and culturally specific, e. g. nodding in agreement, shaking the head in disagreement or raising the shoulders to convey: "I don't know."

8.2 Confining and containing the object of investigation

This paper is looking at motion which conveys meaning, is non-verbal in expression and has a function akin to spoken-language. It must be emphasized that the presented subject of research is a special form of expression; one in a socio-cultural group of conventionalised, non-verbal forms. It is not akin to the sign-language of the deaf: in itself, a unique form of communication and of equal purpose, which does not, however, replace spoken-language in inter-personal communication.

This paper does also not cover "Speech Focused Movements" (Butterworth/Beattie, 1978, 221), which accompany spoken-language statements: "these hand and arm movements appear intimately linked with the process of speech production: they are rhythmically timed with the speech, and often seem to reflect the meaning which the speech expresses." (Butterworth/Beattie, 1978, 347)

See Butterworth & Beattie for a more detailed description and analysis. For an extensive description and clarification of material concerning the dialogue over gesture and meaning, see McNeill (1992).

This paper addresses the spatial form of non-verbal expression as used within a dance context. Such expression is situation- and context-dependent, as opposed to spoken-language driven, and is understood by members of the same 'language-community'.

Signals are consciously sent; non-verbal expression is intentional. To date, relevant literature relating to this special means of bodily expression can only be found concerning Indian dance, of which there is a long tradition of its description and "translation"; albeit overly prescriptive. I can find no written evidence in which it is apparent that this form of expression is an essential part of the music and choreography of traditional African dance. There are two possible reasons:

a) The authors do not understand it or only partially recognise it.
b) It happens very rarely.

To this end and for the first time, I will attempt to:

a) present these special forms of non-verbal expression,
b) clarify them,
c) translate them into the spoken-word and
d) integrate them into some form of semiotic and communication-theoretical framework.

As such, I will attempt to de-marginalise and establish certain prerequisites for the study of traditional African dance.

– In non-verbal expression, the visual, as opposed to the acoustic signal, is the information 'provider'.
– The whole body can potentially be used to convey expression.
– Expression via body-language can be sequential or simultaneous.

In this paper, researched non-verbal expressions will be used, depending on the context, instead of those of the spoken-language. They are conventional symbols and are a part of the overall dance experience.

9. Description of a dance-event from a dance-inherent point of view

Description of human movement can be variously described. Sports Science more or less differentiates between sport-like and non-sport like movement. Descriptive and prescriptive ways of describing movement are distinguished.

Problems can arise because verbally described actions are for the most part incomprehensible. For example, "stamping" is an ambiguous and yet often-used term in African dance literature.

Features of motion can vary greatly even given details of time, space and other such factors.

In addition to my own thoughts, the following conceivable way of describing a dance event draws upon Laban's dance-movement analysis and Klein-Vogelbach's functional dance-training. The following model makes no claim to being exhaustive and the aforementioned problem of ambiguity is not precluded.

The descriptive parameters are:
1. The body as an instrument for dance.
2. The body as space and the space around the body.
3. The direction and planes of movement of the body or parts thereof, the 'operators', in space.
4. The speed of movement and intensity of the 'operator'.
5. Spatial pattern as demonstrated by the 'operator'.
6. Classification of the course of movement, positioning and content, provided they adhere to convention.

The human body is the instrument of performance in the context of dance. Performance here means that the body, or 'operators', move in the room or space and come to a halt in this space, a resting position.

Klein-Vogelbach's terminology governing the naming of body parts and 'operators' will be adopted. They separated the body into functioning parts:
1) head,
2) chest,
3) arm,
4) pelvis and
5) legs.

A more precise description of body parts in relation to the skeleton, coordination points and associated movement, as well as individual body parts, will be looked at in a later chapter.

To describe dance movement, one has to establish the body as being its *own* 'spatial awareness phenomenon' within a given environment. Moreover, the surrounding room has to be defined in relation to directional movement in order to be able to describe the course of events. A thorough description and analysis will then be made possible because the human 'spatial' body can then be established within the context of its surrounding environment.

10. Transcription and notation

Dance motion and motion in general are ephemeral. Attempts have continuously been made to establish a notational system of dance motion. As very little research has been made into it, systems have only been used to assist choreographer and dancer in the memorising of dances. Over a period of time there have been several notation systems, dating as far back as the Renaissance and Baroque eras. Notation from the Renaissance furnishes us with step sequences mostly. Notation was a combination of graphic symbols such as dots, lines and letters. Tempo and spatial environment are not included. Other written details and alterations to the space were also noted. However, dances could not be reconstructed thereafter, given neither the graphic notation provided nor the written description.

Given the great esteem in which dance was held amongst the aristocracy, the book 'Collection of Dances in Choreography Notation' was published in France in 1700.

Graphic symbols plot the floorplan, as further delineated by the movement of dance steps and directional changes. Feuillet's notation contain details about start and end positions and details about foot positioning with accompanying comments about the quality of the dance.

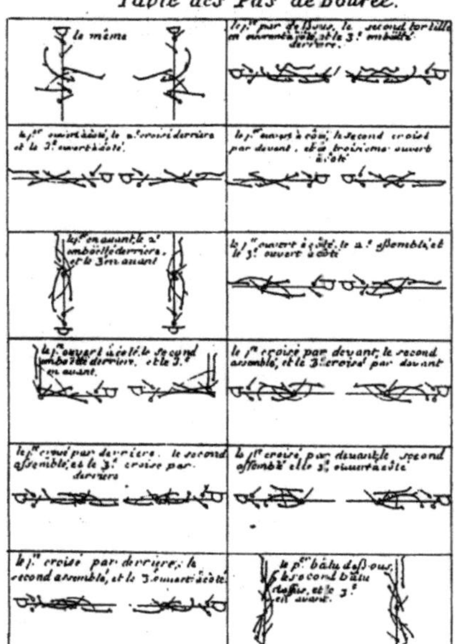

Figure 1 (Voß, 1995)

Dancers such as Mary Wigman, Martha Graham and Kurt Jooss, to mention but a few, have notated their own dances and choreographies. They used symbols, diacritic signs and written notes. Using Mary Wigman's notes as an example, one can show how notation provided the solution to being able to reproduce dances through notated choreography.

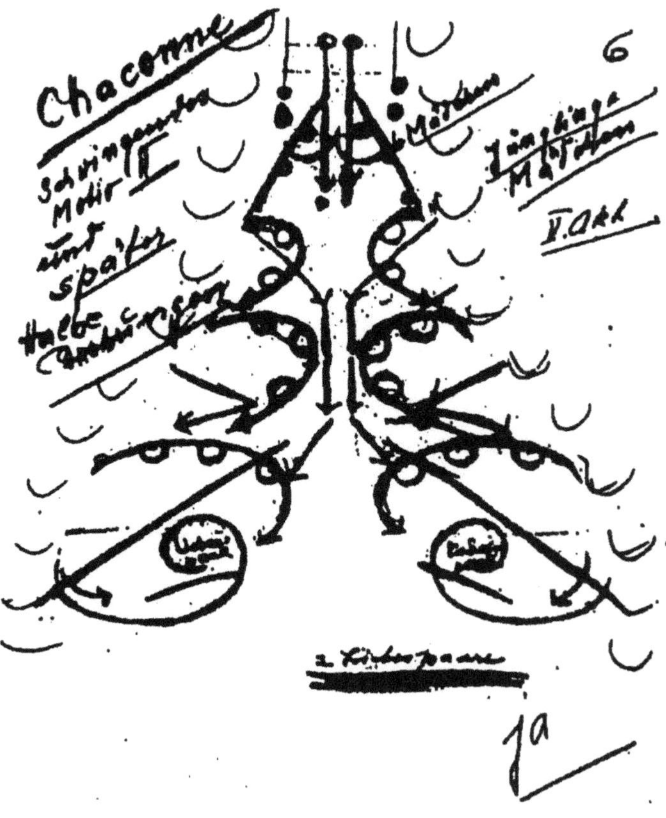

Figure 2 (Wigman, 1963)

Wigman used graphic symbols such as dashes, circles and arrows to denote positioning and direction of movement. She also noted down 'spoken' explanations and used different colours to depict different parts or people (not visible in illustration). Of course, the notation is only readable by, and useful for, the choreographer, not 'outsiders'. The notation is mostly a series of notes and criticisms of the artist over her work. Apart from that, the notation gives no information about the movement itself, rather about the various performing spaces and the locomotion within them.

Only since the subject of dance and motion has become increasingly popular has it become necessary to develop a clearly-defined dance notation system. The systems of Rudolph von Laban and Benesh (Movement Notation), to name but two, are looked at below.

Laban was the pioneer of movement analysis. Originally an architect, he became known as the founder of Modern Dance. His movement analysis system raises the following issues:

1. Relating to the body: muscle tension: gesture, posture, movement onset and progress.
2. Relating to room: position/scope; path of performer's spatial-motion; plane of motion/direction.
3. Relating to the dynamic of motion: Laban differentiates between various-drive factors or 'efforts': focus/space; pressure/power/weight; time/tempo; flow of movement.

He split motion development into, "choreutics spatial", and "eukinetics expressive".

'Kinetography Laban' or 'Labanotation' is widely accepted and used as, "a further development of traditional attempts to notate dance motion using symbols and bases itself on the observation and analysis of movement in time and space." It uses ideographic symbols without text and can only be understood by trained proponents. Direction of reading is from top to bottom.

The notation takes into account:

– the duration of time from motion to motion

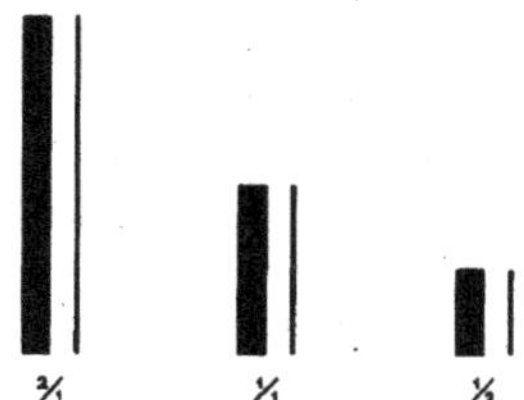

Figure 3 (Laban, 1988)

– symbols showing direction of movement

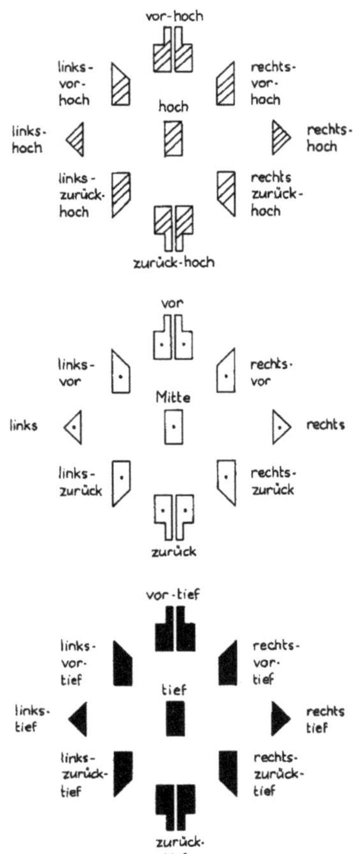

Figure 4 (Laban, 1988)

- symbols showing detail of plane of movement (lower, middle, upper planes)

hohe
mittlere
tiefe
Lage
(Höhe)

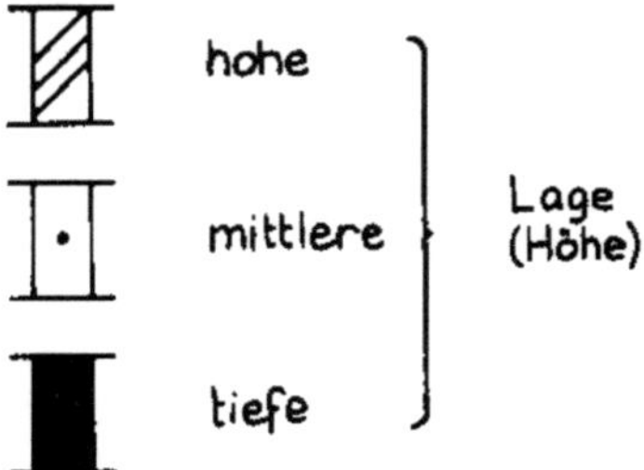

Figure 5 (Laban, 1988)

- symbols recording <u>spatial expanse</u>

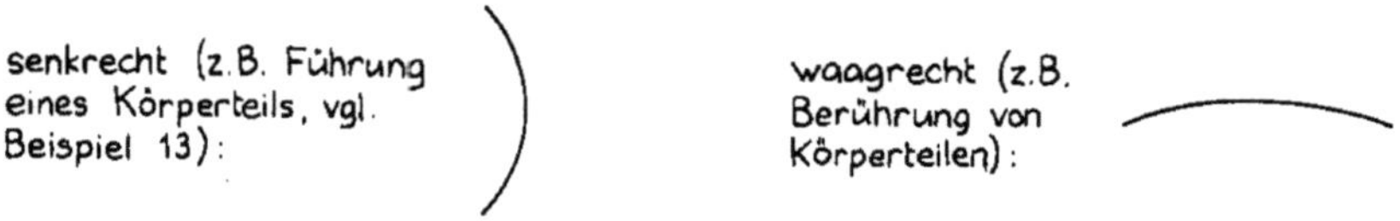

senkrecht (z.B. Führung eines Körperteils, vgl. Beispiel 13):
waagrecht (z.B. Berührung von Körperteilen):

Figure 6 (Laban, 1988)

– symbols governing individual parts of the body

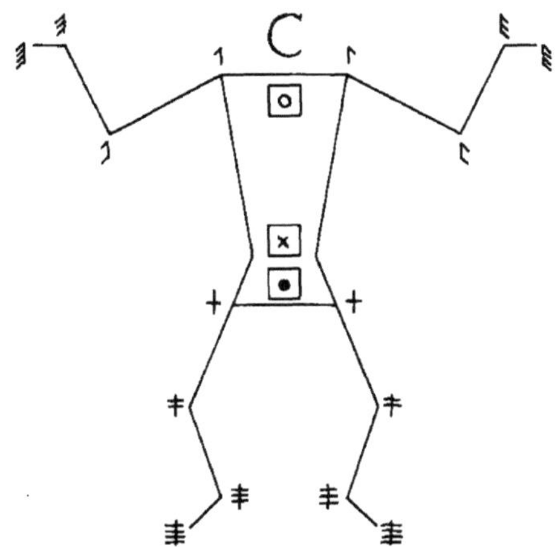

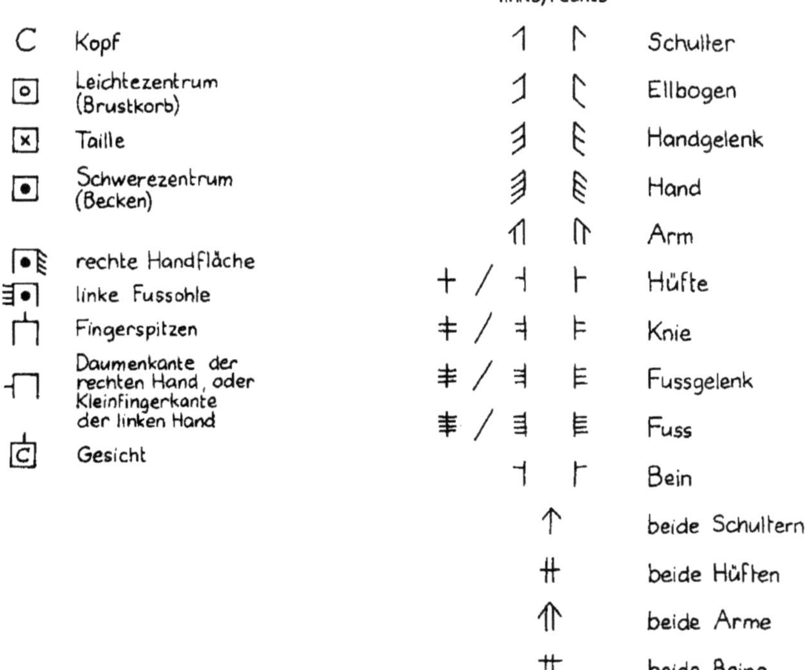

Figure 7 (Laban, 1988)

– extra symbols about transcription of, for example, <u>accent,</u> details over the deviant body part.

Figure 8 (Laban, 1988)

The Benesh Movement Notation is an ideogrammatic script similar to music notation in that it is written over five lines. The five lines delineate body parts and planes: head, shoulders, pelvis, knees and feet (Benesh/Benesh, 1956). There is no correlation between distance between body parts and defined lines. The motion sequence is given using bar-lines and is read from left to right. The following is a transcribed comparison of a 'grand jeté' in Laban and Benesh notation (Benesh/Benesh, 1956).

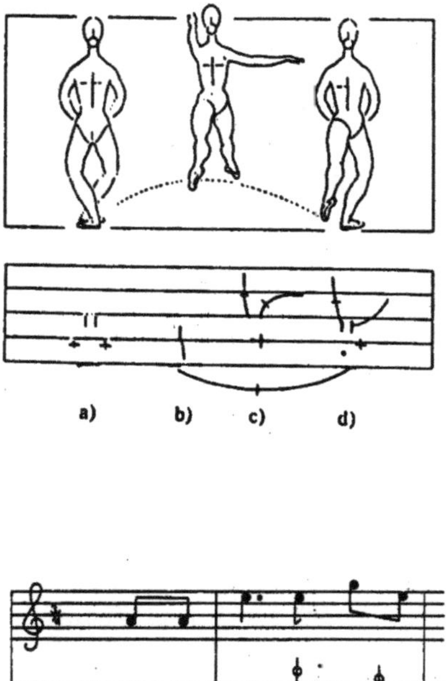

Figure 9 (Laban, 1988)

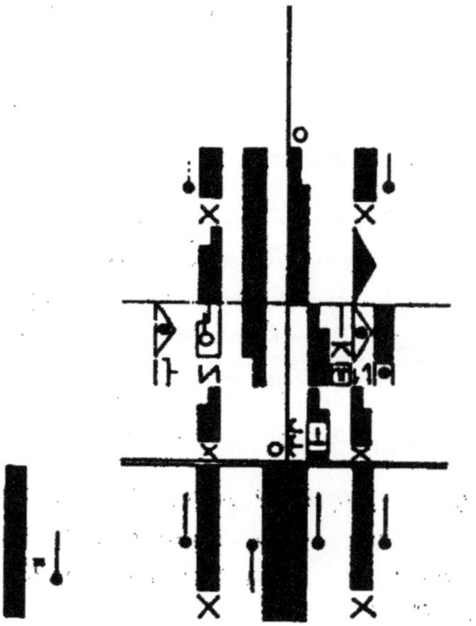

Figure 10 (Laban, 1988)

Comparatively speaking, Laban's notation is both more abstract and more complex. Benesh notation is also abstract but more 'transparent'. The pictogram itself gives the impression of sequential motion and contains segmented sequences of motion. There is a starting point, a transition point relevant to the room (denoting the ideal final position of a jump) and the final position of the dance is displayed. To what extent notation is used depends upon its legibility and the desired outcome. For reasons of legibility and given the objectives of this study, this paper will not be referring to either one of the systems detailed.

11. Evaluation of the data

Data was collated over a five month research period in Ghana. During the visits to Denu and Agbozume (Volta), contact was made with the Department of Music and Dance at the University of Legon and data was collated.

Contributors were
–   the dancers and musicians of the Agbozume dance group and their manager, Kofi Mensah,
–   the dancers and musicians of the Denu dance group and their manager, Adzey Fumey,
–   various interlocutors at the University in Legon and elsewhere.

Aside from data collation, I had to interview many people to amass information concerning content. This was the most difficult part of the process and the most time consuming. Language problems and the dearth of English speakers prompted the hiring of an interpreter. Incompatible cultural norms and values proved to be further obstacles and often led to misunderstanding and misinterpretation. These were subsequently minimised after intense debate. Although the author has many years of practical and theoretical experience of traditional dance west of Africa and other peoples, a thorough appreciation of a foreign socio-cultural milieu is seldom achieved. Ensuing mistakes or misunderstandings are thus likely, for which the author accepts full responsibility.

Data collation comprised:
a) the motion element of the dances,
b) the musical element of the dances.

For technical reasons the dances were not recorded in their usual environments. This raised the quality of audio and visual recording, further helping in the evaluation of gathered material. The author had the opportunity to observe and participate in rehearsals prior to recording, thus learning by observing and doing.

A 45-minute VHS recording was made, partly shot using a wide-angle lens to include:
1) head, trunk, arms and legs in their entirety,
2) movement and directional change of movement,
3) any changes in the plane of movement.

Two takes were made of each dance to allow for any changes and to guarantee the thoroughness of material.

We recorded using DAT and via the camcorder microphone. Rhythmic patterning was notated using a 'logatom'. Music and motion material are fully integrated. Musical material will not be evaluated as it does not come within the scope of this paper.

Questions of content and of a historical and contextual nature were asked during and around the time of the recordings. Non-linguistic problems were talked out with participants at great length. The text was notated in Ewe, Fon and translated into German. Drum text is in Ewe.

Video material was processed at the computer centre and Institute of Phonetics in Cologne and viewed using Adobe Premiere on a MAC system. The signal was at first sectioned and then digitalised, subsequent subdivisions being singularly viewed and then possibly further sub-divided.

The resulting 'items' (positions):
- are segments in which one or more of the 'operators' change direction.
- There are interruptions/pauses in the signal/sequence of music and dance.
- There are no pauses during changes of movement.
- Other movement sequences are introduced.

Established positions were then printed using 'Adobe Photoshop', described, analysed and notated as pictograms. A conceptualised schema was chosen to represent the body with the various functional body segments (= BS. Klein-Vogelbach, 1990, 74ff.) in mind.

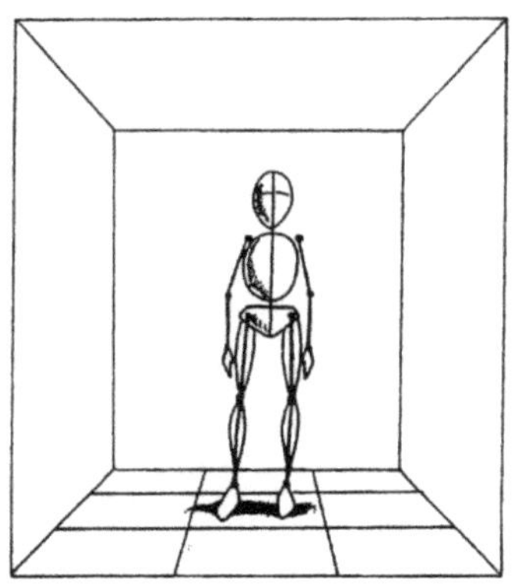

Figure 11

Joints were marked using dots. A more detailed description follows in section 9.

11.1 Explanation of material

The Adzogbo dance is part of a trilogy: Agbadja, Agbeko (= Adzagbeko) and
Adzogbo. All three are traditional war dances.

'Agbadja'
During periods of war this dance was used for relaxation. Nowadays it is only
danced at burials, otherwise "someone could die".

'Agbeko'
An after-war dance which was originally danced to explain the history of mi-
gration of the Ewe, including the various conflicts experienced underway.
Nowadays used in schools to document the story of migration.

'Adzogbo'
Dates from the 18th century coastal regions. It was danced prior to battle to
embed a code of conduct and confer a sense of spiritual strength. Apart from
that, it was a kind of strength and endurance for warriors. These dances were
brought to Denu years ago. A traditional dance teacher was brought in from
Benin as the local christianised population had come to regard the dance as
'voodoo' and no one wanted to have anything more to do with it. Nowadays
it is danced at competitions, music festivals, births, deaths and as a means of
relaxation. In its entirety, it is a chronology of ten self-contained sequences, originally danced exclusively by men but nowadays by women too. It is
danced anti-clockwise, in a circle with the musicians in the middle.

The orchestra bases itself upon percussive instruments, the atsimevu, sogo,
kagan, kidi and the double Gatingo-bell. All drums are played with sticks.
The bell keeps the time throughout the piece. The sogo, kagan and kidi
drums accompany the lead drum, the atsimevu, which is responsible for
drumming the dance-text.

Atsimevu means 'sitting drum' and accordingly 'sits' on the ground in a
wooden frame. It is 1.5 m long and is played in a sitting position.

The music is 'polymetric' (Chernoff, 1994, 67). The onset is not achieved
by counting bars but rather with reference to the playing of other instruments. The western concept of pulse and main beat is not apparent and the
western ear, attuned as such, may not be able to orientate itself to the rhythmic complexity. "The changeable attribute of Ewe drumming is so well tak-
en advantage of by the master drummer, that one has the impression of time
being 'stretched' or contracted." (Chernoff, 1994, 69) When played together,

the outwardly simple rhythms of the Adzogbo come across to the untrained ear as unstructured and chaotic. The dancer has to take on board the varying rhythms and translate them into 'corporal polycentricity'. He coordinates his use of foot gesturing through the ongoing rhythm of the bell. The enduring patterns are displayed using the individual movement centres. Independently mobile parts of the body move in response to these rhythmic patterns (Chernoff, 1994, 68). These can be the throat, upper thorax, upper body as a whole, the arms or hips.

Synchronicity between dancer and musician is a criterion for good dancing (and musicianship). The ability of a dancer to 'consume' the rhythmic structure and interpret 'text' is also a sign of quality. Dancer and musician are interdependent. The 'talking drum' of the master drummer will reflect any inability on the part of the dancer. Just as a good dancer orientates himself to the music, so too does the good musician orientate himself to the dancer's feet.

> "Regular, changeable rhythm is controlled by the 'feeling' of the drummer: he plays what he feels. People sometimes dance when he plays. He observes their body movements and that of their feet, and depending upon the way the dancer chooses to move, the drummer will accompany him. So I say, you should have got a Takai dancer and drummer to study on their own, because you would have seen someone who knows how to move his feet and a drummer who really observes the dancer. When the dancer raises his feet and moves his body, the drummer plays exactly the right kind of rhythm. You can then clearly see just how both fit together and how rhythm changes match the type of dance." (Chernoff, 1994, 135)

Just to clarify that the quote does not imply free improvisation between musician and dancer. It is more to do with changes of style (Chernoff, 1994, 136) in a piece, within which framework the musician and the dancer are able to improvise. If the musician and dancer are well warmed-up, the piece will be danced and played 'by itself'.

Relating to the Adzogbo one can say that:
- The dance, as described, is not possible without accompaniment. An evaluation of the rhythmic structure is, however, not the objective of this paper.
- The atsimevu (Talking Drum) drummer plays the text.
- The dancer absorbs the 'spoken music' sequences and translates them into 'spoken dance'.
- Musician and dancer are bound together by rhythmic patterns and the dance-text.

11.2 Evaluation of 'motion data'

The explanation of material is made possible with the use of several personal, and the following descriptive, methods:

a) Klein-Vogelbach's (1993) functional kinetics and
b) Elements of Laban's models (Laban, 1988).

Only procedures and terminology relevant to this study have been made use of.

Functional kinetics is a procedure based upon functional anatomy and further developed in the field of physiotherapy.
The body has been divided into functional body segments as follows (Klein-Vogelbach, 1993, 74ff.):
1) BS head: sensory organs and brain with accompanying skeletal parts, seven discs of the cervical spinal vertebrae, skull and lower jaw-bone

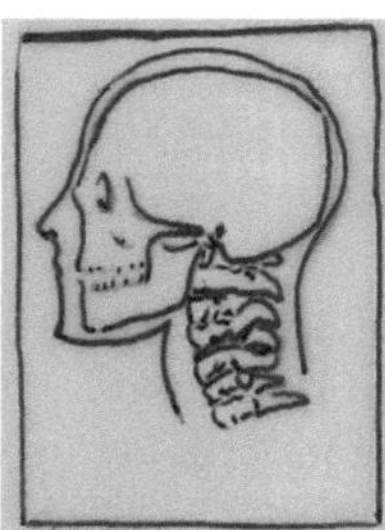

Figure 12 (According to Klein-Vogelbach, 1993)

2) BS thorax and twelve vertebrae of the thoracic spinal column, twelve pairs of ribs and sternum

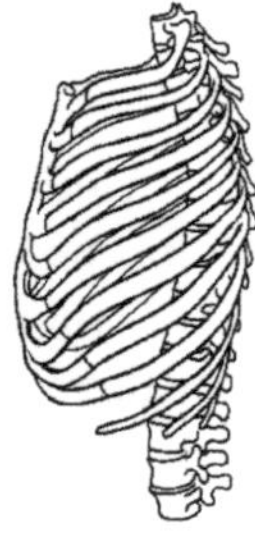

Figure 13 (Klein-Vogelbach, 1993)

3) Pelvis and five vertebrae of the lumbar spinal column, the sacrum and both ossa coxae. The pelvis maintains the balance between thorax and pelvis. Thorax and pelvis perform 'different functions'. The alternating locomotor activity of the legs is controlled and coordinated from the pelvis and transmitted onto the spinal column.

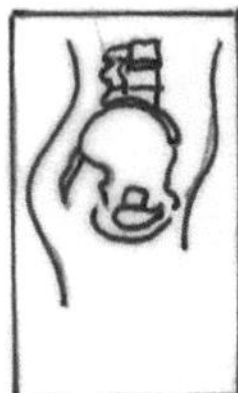

Figure 14 (According to Klein-Vogelbach, 1993)

4) Arms and left and right clavicle, scapula, left and right humerus left and right ulna, ossa carpi, navicular bone, trapezius major and minor, pisiform bone, lunate bone, the triquetrum, capitate bone, hamate bone, five metacarpalis, five phalanges.

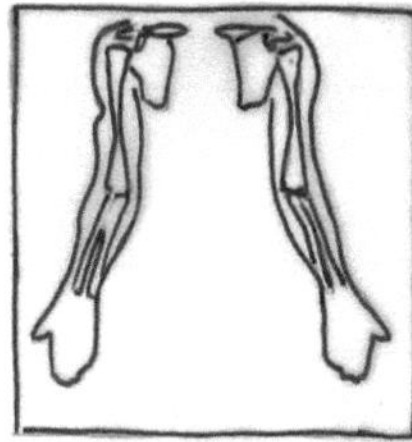

Figure 15 (According to Klein-Vogelbach, 1993)

5) Legs and related skeletal parts: left and right femur, l and r tibia, fibula l and r talus, calcaneus, navicular bone, os cuboideum, 3 os cuneiformes, 5 metatarsal bones, 5 phalanges. The legs provide, amongst other things, locomotion.

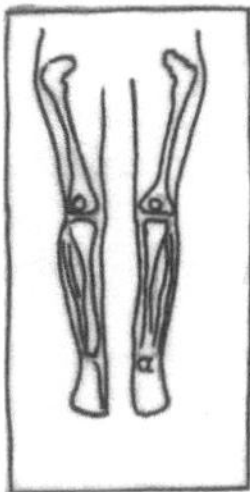

Figure 16 (According to Klein-Vogelbach, 1993)

11.3 Basic movement

In functional movement theory, the co-ordinating points or joints are paramount. They are the members which join the two substantial body parts together and enable movement. Relevant to the tables below, the following joints and related movement are to be identified:
-   shoulder, elbow, hand, hip, knee, foot
-   flexion, extension, abduction, adduction, rotation, pronation and supination (Görner, 1992; Klein-Vogelbach, 1993).

	Flexion	**Extension**
Shoulders	arm raised forwards	arm raised backwards
Elbow	bending	stretching
Wrist	palm towards underarm	stretching
Pelvis	raise leg forwards	raise leg backwards, toes up to knee
Knee joint	heel to seat	stretching
Ankle	toes down to floor	toes up to knee

Table 3

	Abduction	**Adduction**
Shoulder	sideways lift of arm	sideways dropping of arm
Pelvis	sideways extension	raise leg
Wrist	*ulnare abduction:* little finger toward underarm *radial abduction:* thumb towards underarm	

Table 4

	Pronation	**Supination**
Hand and Elbow	palm downwards	palm upwards
Ankle	inner sole towards knee	outer sole to knee

Table 5

	Rotation
Cervical spine (CS)	Rotating of the head around a virtual axis through the cervical spine
Shoulder joint	Rotating of the arm around the longitudinal axis of the upper arm
Hip joint	Rotating of the leg around the longitudinal axis of the thigh
Knee joint	Rotating of the lower leg and foot around the longitudinal axis of the lower leg

Table 6

Mobility of the vertebrae

	Ventral flexion	Dorsal flexion	Lateral flexion	Rotation
Cervical spine	+	+	+	+
Thoracic spine	+	+	+	+
Lumbar spine	+	+	+	+

Table 7

The degree of flexibility in each vertebra varies. Flexion of the cervical verte-brae is, for example, greater than that of the thorax.

11.4 Bodily and spatial orientation

People orientate their own personal-space within room-space, as does a per-former. Kinaesthetic perception, particularly inward-sensitivity, brings about personal positioning. Governed by changes in individual 'operators', it also enables a self-orientation process. It also governs the positioning of body parts, gaps between body parts and a perception of direction as effected by the various operators (Klein-Vogelbach, 1993, 3ff.). The vertical displacement of a body in space is a constant, as determined by gravity (Klein-Vogelbach, 1993, 6).

In an upright position the body orientates itself in a space using its field of vision. Furthermore, in <u>coordination</u> terms we include the reference sys-tem *left* and *right*, and *in front of* and *behind*.

For the <u>placement</u> of an individual we denote: *in front, behind, left* and *right*.

For the <u>movement</u> of the individual: *forwards, backwards, to the left, to the right*.

In summary, we can consider:
- because of constant gravity, a 'position' up and down, and the 'directions' upwards and downwards.
- from the individual's field of vision, the 'positions' left/right/in front of/ behind and the 'directions', to the left/to the right/forwards and backwards.

11.5 Orientation of observers

To fully describe the aforementioned movement data it is necessary to derive a reference system from the observer's point of view. The performer is positioned in an abstract space, a cube.

The descriptive parameters established are:

Transversal, frontal and sagittal planes
The figure is in a cube. The planes of the cube interrelate with the body.

Transversal plane
The upper plane relates to the crown of the head, the lower plane to the ground under the figure's feet. The various transversal planes between the two correlate to the various parts of the body.

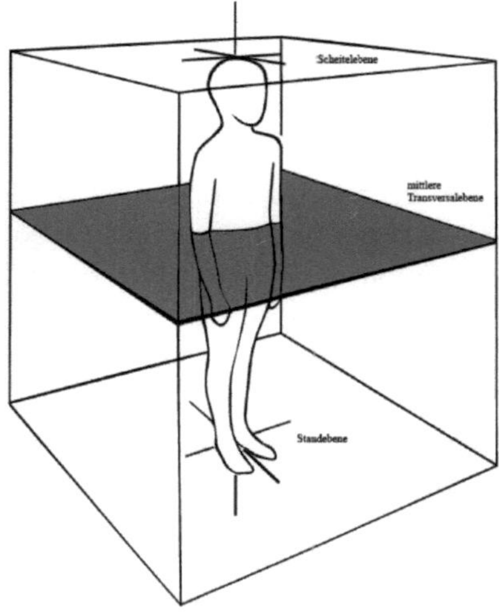

Figure 17 (According to Klein-Vogelbach, 1993)

The lower transversal plane is referred to as 'ground-level', the upper as the 'apex'. The middle is called the 'middle transverse level'.

Above the middle plane is the 'cranial segment', below it the caudal.

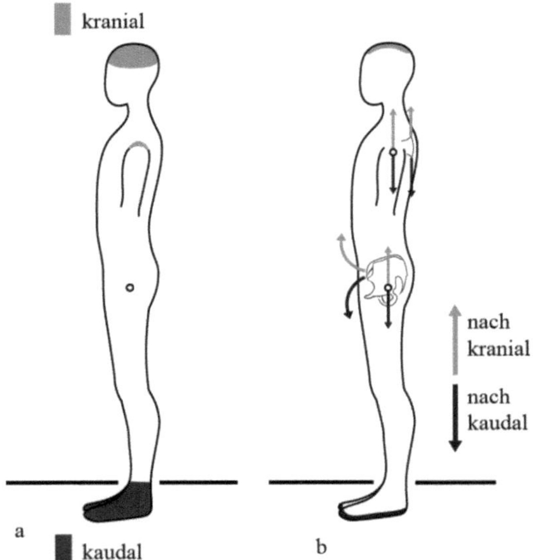

Figure 18 (According to Klein-Vogelbach, 1993)

Summary:
– Positional details: cranial, caudal
– Directional details: towards the head, towards the feet.

Frontal plane

In front of and behind the body is referred to as the O-position. Parallel planes relating to the O-position are called 'frontal planes'.

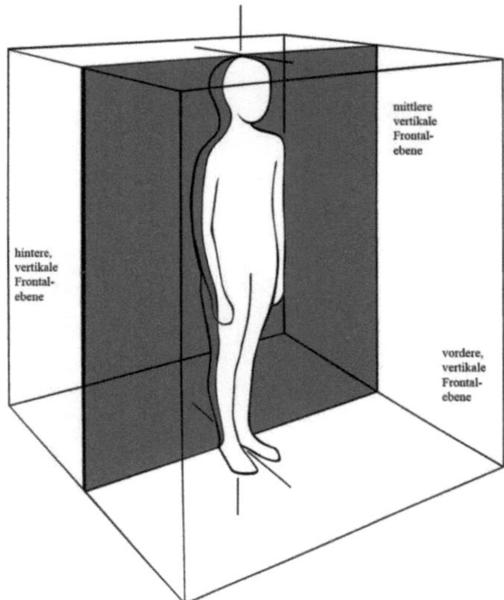

Figure 19 (According to Klein-Vogelbach, 1993)

These also relate to the body. They are subdivided into 'ventral' (abdominal) and 'dorsal' (spinal).

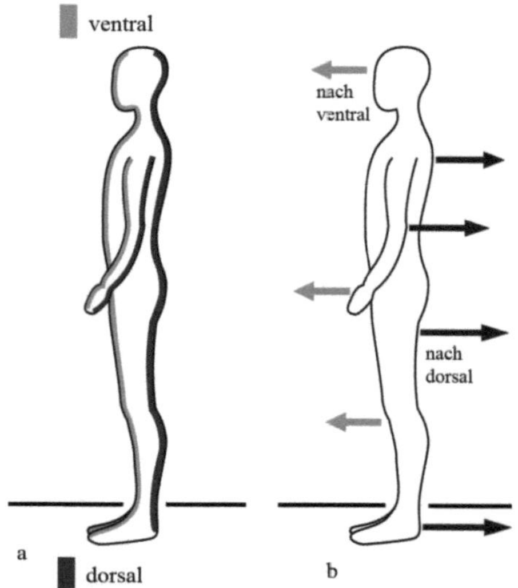

Figure 20 (According to Klein-Vogelbach, 1993)

The frontal plane cutting through the middle is the 'middle-frontal plane'.
- Positional details: ventral (abdominal), dorsal (spinal)
- Directional details: towards the abdomen, towards the back

Sagittal plane

Those planes between the left and right sides are 'sagittal' planes. They split the body into left-lateral and right-lateral.

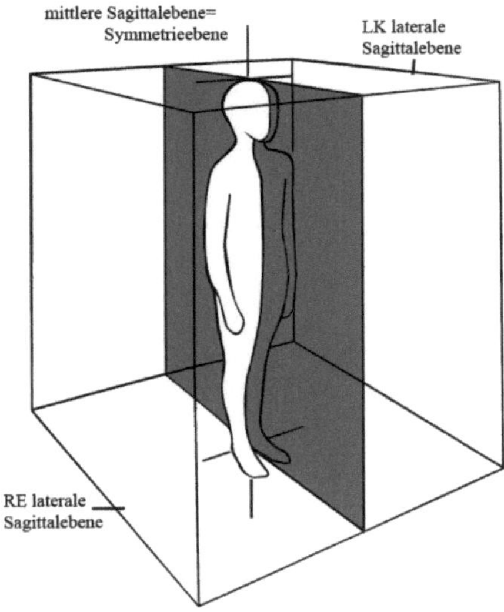

Figure 21 (According to Klein-Vogelbach, 1993)

The sagittal plane passing through the middle of the body is the 'symmetrical', 'median' or 'middle-sagittal' plane. "It splits the body into symmetrical left and right parts." (Klein-Vogelbach, 1993, 23)

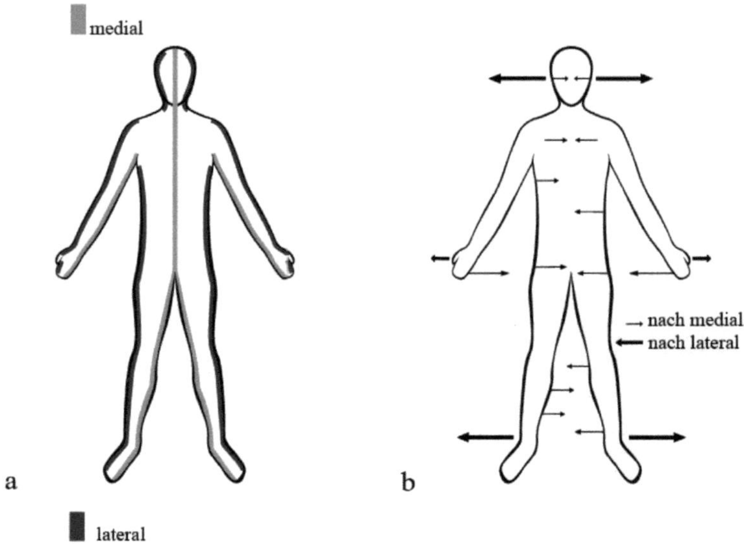

Figure 22 (According to Klein-Vogelbach, 1993)

Summary:
- Positional details: lateral (on the side), left-lateral, right-lateral and medial.
- Directional details: to the side, to the left side, to the right side, to the medial.

Vertex and longitudinal axis

"Definition: The vertex is the point of intersection between the symmetrical, middle-frontal and apex planes. The longitudinal axis is the intersecting line between symmetrical and middle-frontal planes. It goes through the middle of the body and the apex." (Klein-Vogelbach, 1993, 26)

It is a virtual axis, corresponding to the spinal column. "It is a virtual axis, definable when the spine is in its neutral position, as the line between pelvis, chest and head." (Klein-Vogelbach, 1993, 26)

11.6 Establishing the space

The description of dance within a room requires the determination of an abstract space with dimensions and directions as defined relating to the room.

The room is established with three dimensions: in front-behind (x), left-right (y) and up-down (z) and six resulting directions. Unrelated to the position and orientation of the body, these parameters remain constant. Using theatre convention, by which I mean, as if standing on stage and looking out into the auditorium, we have the following positional details:

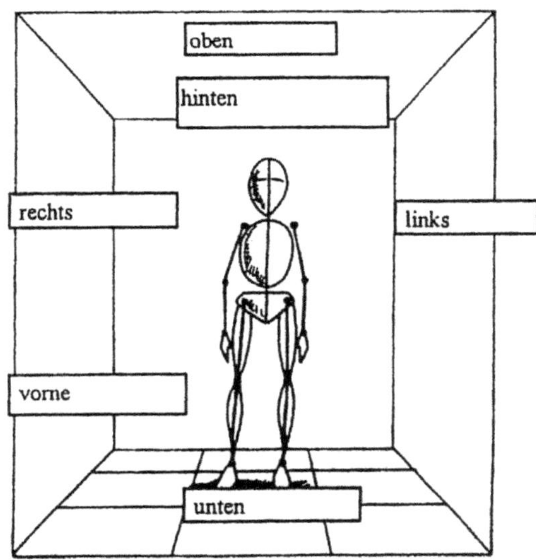

Figure 23

Positional details (topographic):

Directional details:

11.7 Classification of bodily movements

The following is a description of movement sequences relating to dance:

Locomotion
'Steps'
a) Whole step: Both legs move through the middle-vertical-frontal plane towards the ventral or dorsal. A redistribution of weight from one leg to the other occurs.
b) Half step: One-legged step, the other, for example, from dorsal to medial.

Turn
A 'turn' is a rotation through the vertical longitudinal axis, whereby
a) one foot takes half a step. The ankle on the other foot is raised and a rotation along the longitudinal axis of the pivot leg occurs; either to the left or the right.
b) both feet remain on the floor, performer goes onto the balls of the feet and turns (body-weight redistributes to either ventral or dorsal planes).

Jump
Both feet lose contact with the floor for a certain duration. Different to a step in that, at any one time, only *one* foot loses contact with the floor. A jump can be made through the vertical frontal plane,
– on the spot
– legs to the front and back simultaneously.
A two-legged jump can be landed on one or both feet.

Rotary jump
This is a complete rotation through the vertical body axis, whereby both legs leave the ground for a short time. It can be a 90° (1/4), 180° (1/2), 270° (3/4) or 360° (full) turn. It is a rotation through the left lateral (in the room: front, to the left, behind, to the right, front) or the right (room: front, to the right, behind, to the left, front).

Other moves
1. High seat: Pelvis: From neutral, left and right hips are brought close to left and right ankles. Maximum flexion in hip and knee joints.
2. Half crouch

11.8 Corporal segmentation, notation and description thereof

The process of notation and description can be simplified as follows:

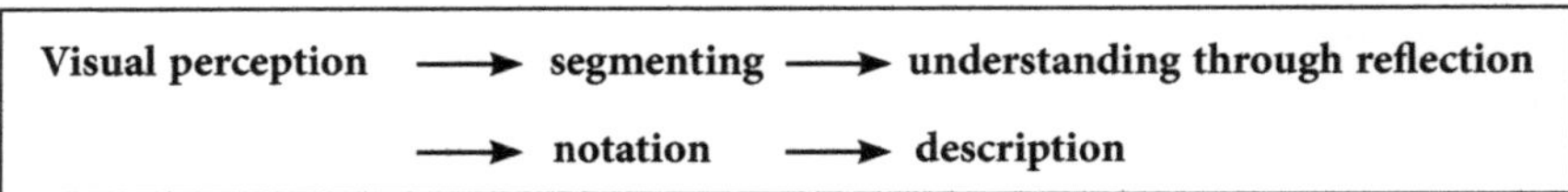

The dance produces a motion continuum (= dancing). The 'Adzogbo' can be split in various ways:
1) as a complete self-contained unit.
2) as a series of sequences and intervals. Each sequence is a self-contained unit, and has its own characteristic text. Sequences are linked to one another with commensurate intervals. All the sequences put together make up the dance.
3) A sequence can be segmented into smaller units. Together, the units make up a sequence.
    The units are the conversion:
    a) of the aforementioned acoustic signals into physical-rhythmic motion (**rhythmic gesture**).
    b) of the aforementioned acoustic (drum-language), textualised signals into physical, scenario-based motion (**textual gesture**).
4) A unit of motion can be further split into smaller segments. Criteria governing the position of the cut within the continuum are:
    1. changes in position or direction of one or more of the 'operators',
    2. initial, end and interim position within a motion.

In other words:

Sub-divided segments are indications of which one or more of the 'operators' change direction.

Established segments will be presented as 'idealised positions' which are, however, not realistically achievable. Segment description will be carried out in the above fashion and will relate only to those features which are significant. A description will be made using anatomical parameters.

Presentation is in image form, followed by the use of pictograms, in which head, thorax, pelvis, arms and legs are schematically displayed. Joints will be emphasized using dots and the spine via a drawn line.

For technical reasons not every segment position can be displayed in pictogram-form. To clarify the course of an 'operators' movements, symbols will be used where relevant (see sect. 9, Figure 8).

Linear pictograms run from left to right (see 10, Figure 1–12) and, as such, depict a time axis. Time-lapse is, however, not easy to distinguish. Properties of longevity and intensity of motion will not be taken into account. The method of describing and notating rhythmical phrasing of motion will also not be considered.

12. Describing the various positions

The pictograms will be presented first, followed by the relevant description.

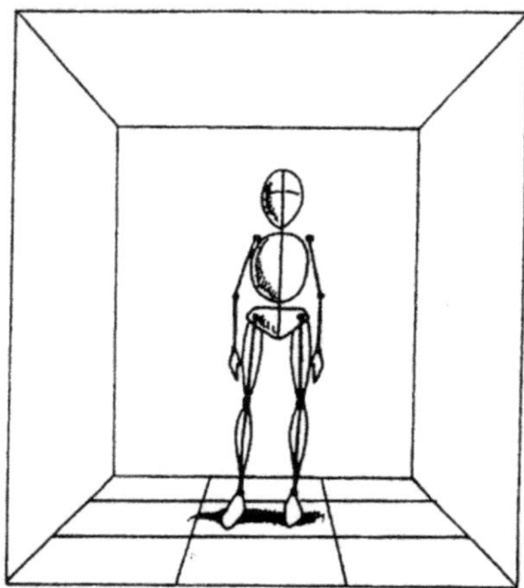

Figure 24

O-position or 'neutral' (Debrunner, 1971)

Aspect: From the ventral, all joints in the O-position (**medial position**)

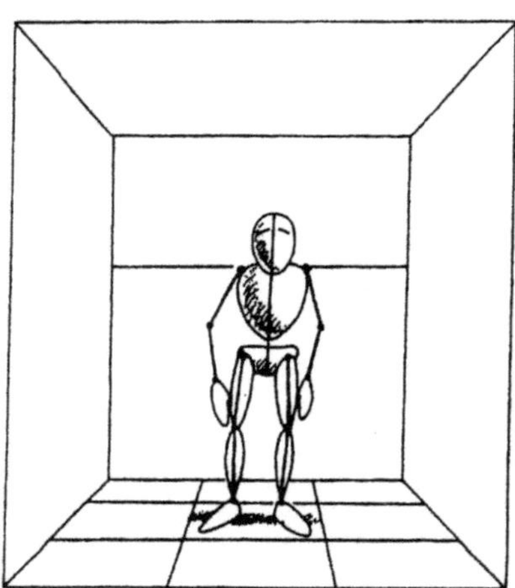

Figure 25

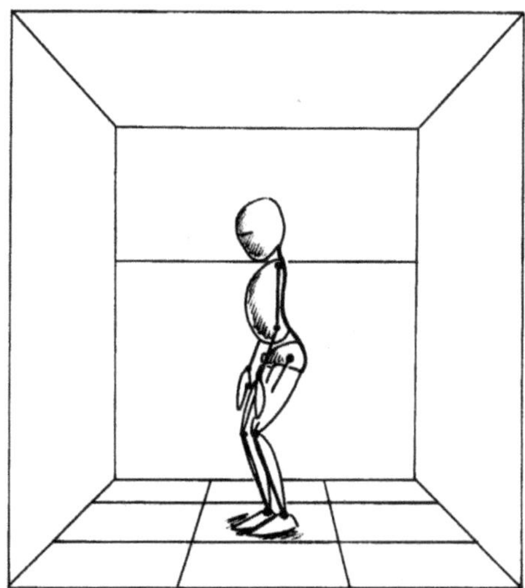

Figure 26

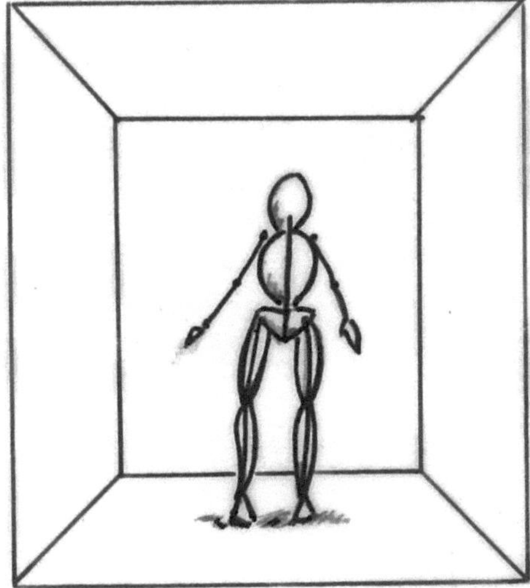

Figure 27

Figures 25–27

Aspect	from ventral, from left lateral, from dorsal
BS head	
BS thorax	anti-flexion (flexion towards ventral)
BS arms	
BS pelvis	extension
BS legs	medial position (neither abducted nor adducted)
Longitudinal axis	
Cervical vertebrae	
Shoulder joint	
Elbow joint	
Wrist	
Hip joint	l: flexion, r: flexion
Knee joint	l: flexion, r: flexion
Ankle	

This position can be described as the 'basic position' or 'basic posture' as it is the starting point of every sequence. Basic posture means the ability to hold this position for a sustained period of time. Certain body parts are more significant than others, which can be used to carry out other actions. In the above position, the legs could also be making steps and turns, while the arms could be doing something else (see, e. g. Figure 11).

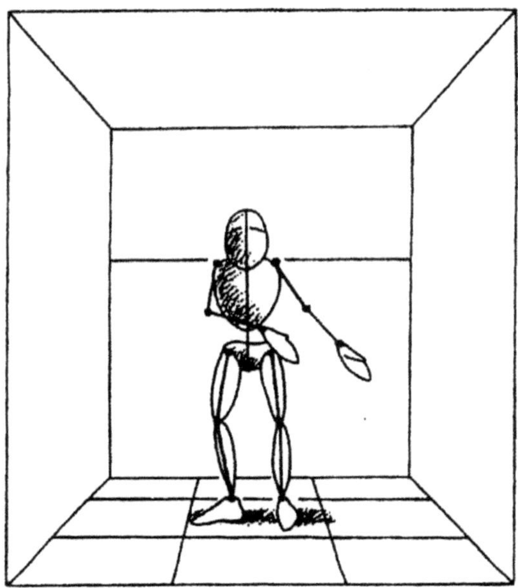

Figure 28

Aspect	from ventral
Head	
Thorax	
Arms	
Pelvis	
Legs	
Longitudinal axis	rotation towards right lateral
Cervical vertebrae	
Shoulder	l: adduction, outward rotation, r: adduction, inward rotation
Elbow	r: supination; flexion on the frontal plane
Wrist	
Hip	r: outward rotation, abduction, flexion
Knee	r: inflected
Ankle	

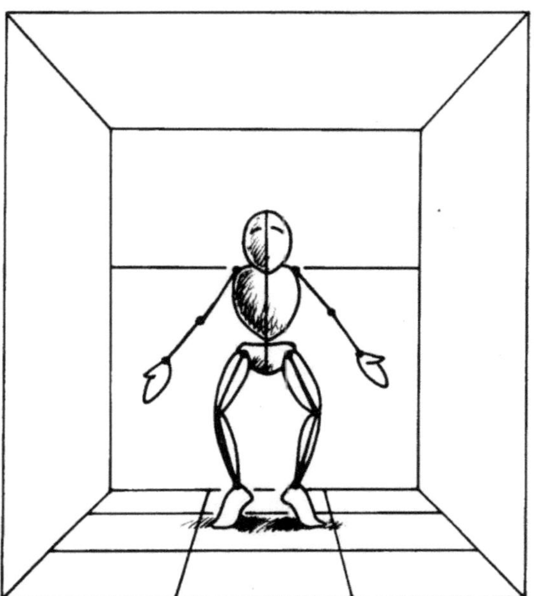

Figure 29

Aspect	from ventral
Head	
Thorax	
Arms	
Pelvis	
Legs	
Longitudinal axis	
Cervical vertebrae	
Shoulder	l: adduction, outward rotation, r: adduction, outward rotation,
Elbow	
Wrist	
Hip	
Knee	
Ankle	l: flexion, r: flexion

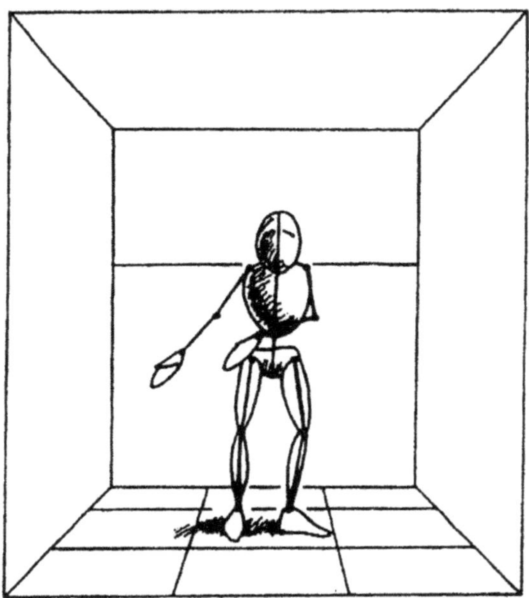

Figure 30

Aspect	from ventral
Head	
Thorax	
Arms	
Pelvis	
Legs	
Longitudinal axis	
Cervical vertebrae	
Shoulder	l: adduction, inward rotation, r: adduction, outward rotation,
Elbow	l: flexion on the frontal plane
Wrist	
Hip	
Knee	
Ankle	

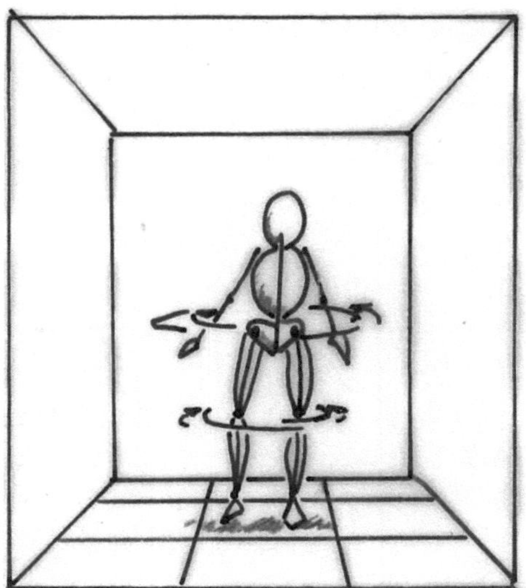

Figure 31

Turn from O-position over left-behind-right into O-position, then from O-position to right-behind-left

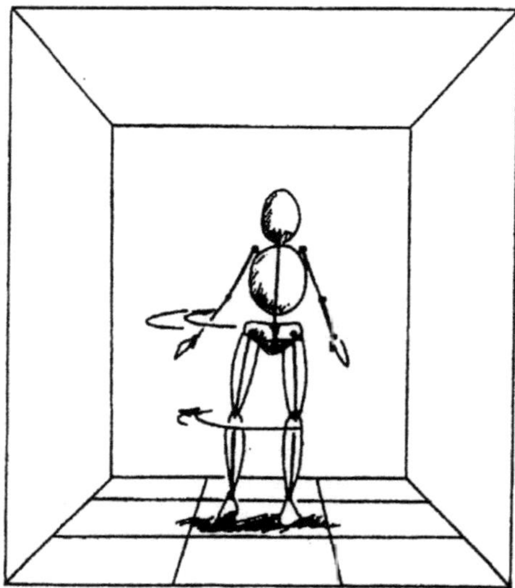

Figure 32

Turn from O-position to right-left-behind

80

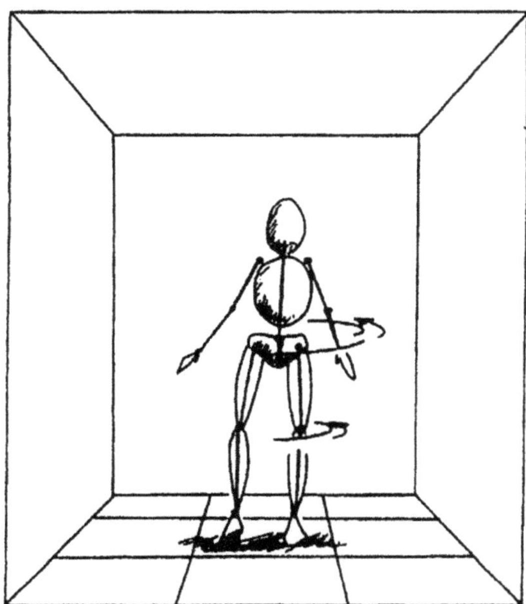

Figure 33

Turn from O-position to left-behind-right

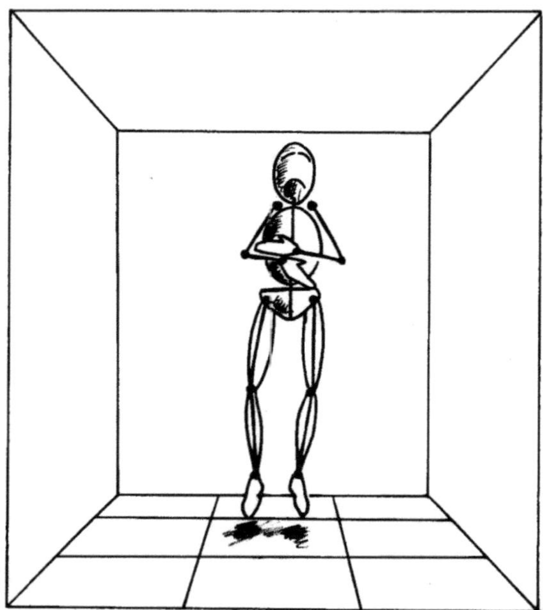

Figure 34

Aspect	from ventral
Head	
Thorax	
Arms	
Pelvis	
Legs	jump
Longitudinal axis	
Cervical vertebrae	extension
Shoulder	
Elbow	l: flexion on the frontal plane, r: flexion on the frontal plane
Wrist	
Hip	
Knee	mid-way
Ankle	flexion

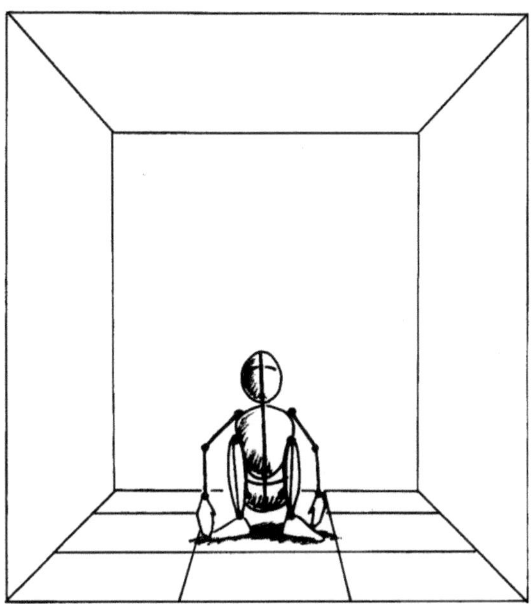

Figure 35

Aspect	from ventral
Head	
Thorax	extension
Arms	
Pelvis	flexion, crouched
Legs	
Longitudinal axis	
Cervical vertebrae	
Shoulder	
Elbow	
Wrist	
Hip	
Knee	flexion
Ankle	

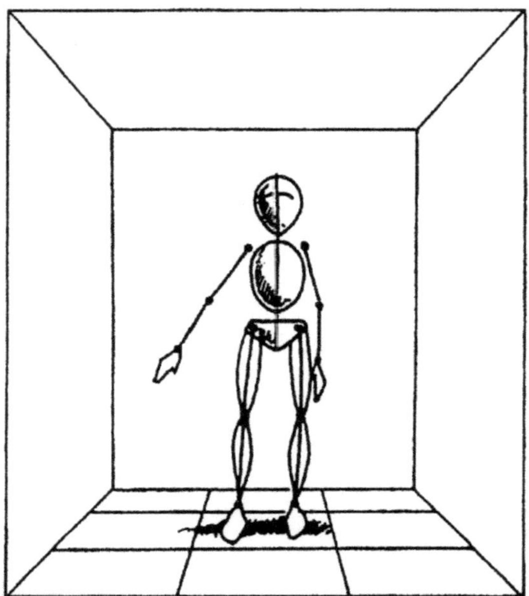

Figure 36

Aspect	from ventral
Head	
Thorax	
Arms	
Pelvis	
Legs	
Longitudinal axis	
Cervical vertebrae	
Shoulder	r: abduction, 45
Elbow	
Wrist	
Hip	
Knee	
Ankle	

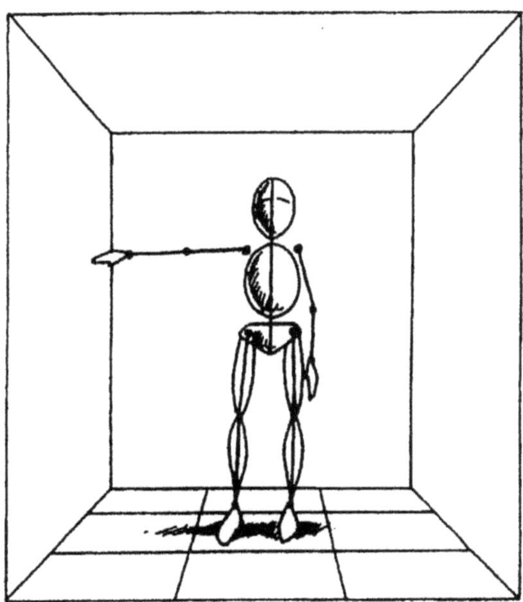

Figure 37

Aspect	from ventral
Head	
Thorax	
Arms	
Pelvis	
Legs	
Longitudinal axis	
Cervical vertebrae	
Shoulder	r: abduction, 90
Elbow	
Wrist	
Hip	
Knee	
Ankle	

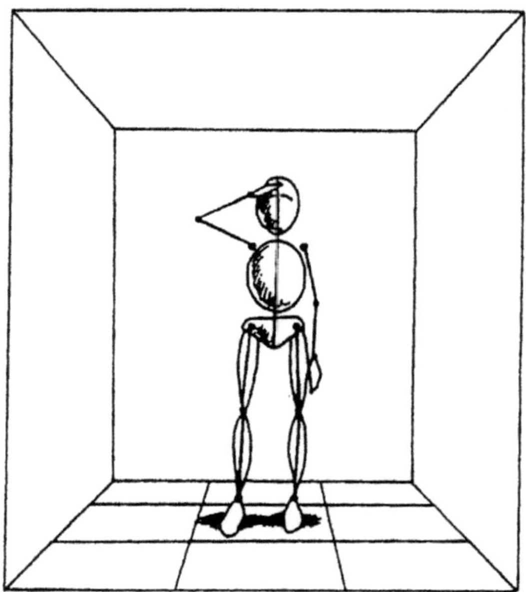

Figure 38

Aspect	from ventral
Head	
Thorax	
Arms	right index finger touches the centre of the forehead
Pelvis	
Legs	
Longitudinal axis	
Cervical vertebrae	
Shoulder	r: abduction,
Elbow	r: flexion
Wrist	
Hip	
Knee	
Ankle	

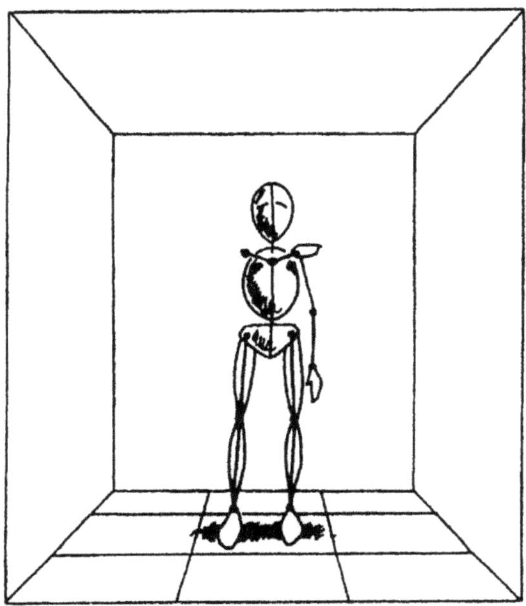

Figure 39

Aspect	from ventral
Head	
Thorax	
Arms	movement of the right arm on the transversal plane
Pelvis	
Legs	
Longitudinal axis	
Cervical vertebrae	
Shoulder	r: abduction via elevation
Elbow	r: flexion
Wrist	
Hip	
Knee	
Ankle	

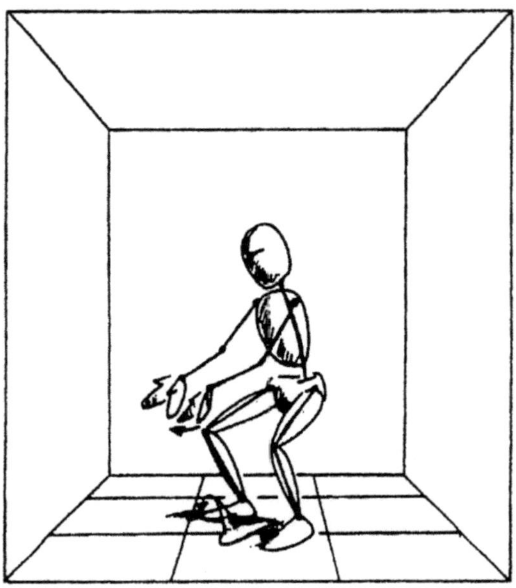

Figure 40

Aspect	from diagonal left
Head	
Thorax	truncal rotation
Arms	
Pelvis	
Legs	
Longitudinal axis	
Cervical vertebrae	
Shoulder	l: flexion, r: flexion
Elbow	l: flexion, supination; r: flexion, supination
Wrist	l: supination, flexion – radial abduction – extension
	l: supination, flexion – radial abduction - extension
Hip	l: flexion, outwards rotation - abduction:
Knee	l: flexion; r: flexion
Ankle	

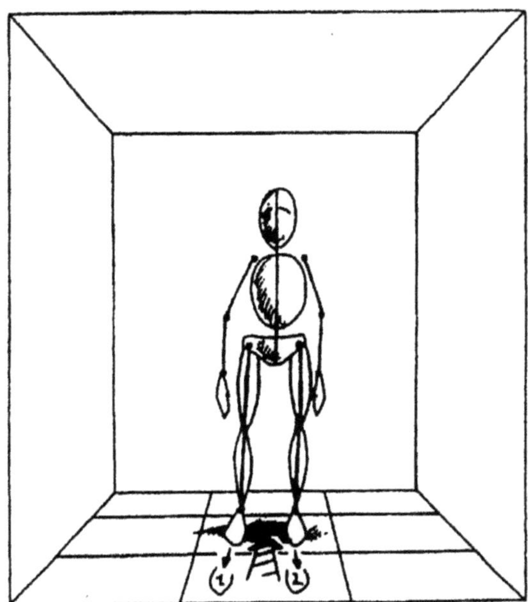

Figure 41

Depiction of a course of movement using diacritical symbols which clearly show directional movement (forwards/backwards)

Aspect	from ventral
Head	
Thorax	
Arms	
Pelvis	
Legs	1. whole step – front right; half step front left
	2. jump backwards in O-position
Longitudinal axis	
Cervical vertebrae	
Shoulder	
Elbow	
Wrist	
Hip	
Knee	
Ankle	

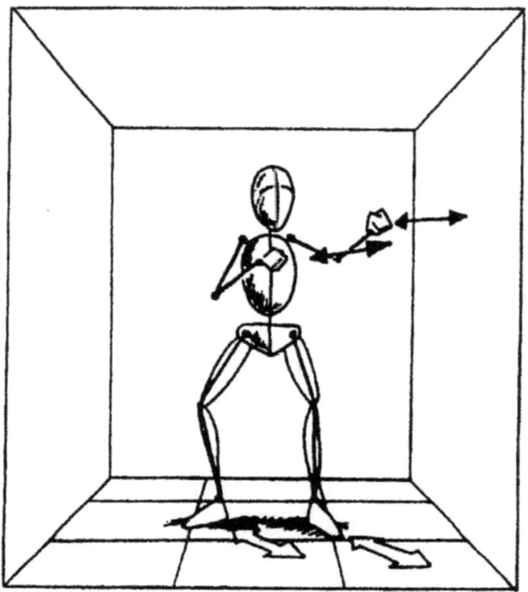

Figure 42

Aspect	from ventral
Head	
Thorax	
Arms	boxing, alternating
Pelvis	
Legs	
Longitudinal axis	rotation lateral left
Cervical vertebrae	rotation to the left
Shoulder	l: abduction; r: abduction
Elbow	l: flexion; r: flexion
Wrist	
Knuckles	flexion
Hip	
Knee	
Ankle	

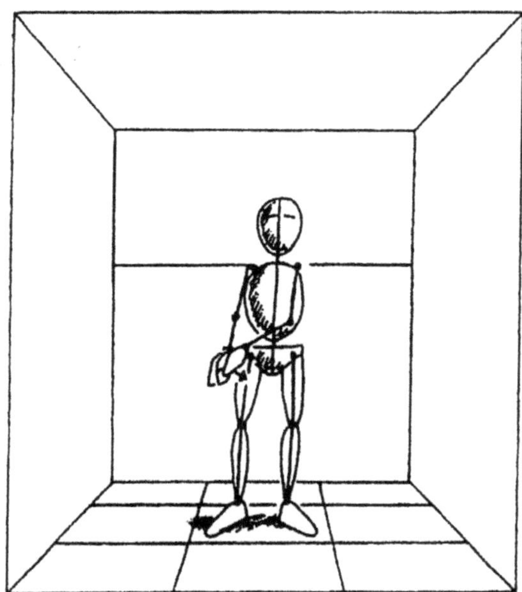

Figure 43

Aspect	from ventral
Head	
Thorax	
Arms	
Pelvis	
Legs	
Longitudinal axis	
Cervical vertebrae	
Shoulder	l: abduction; r: abduction
Elbow	l: flexion on the frontal plane; r: flexion on the frontal plane
Wrist	l: flexion and extension (gradual, repetitive)
	l: flexion and extension (gradual, repetitive)
Hip	
Knee	
Ankle	

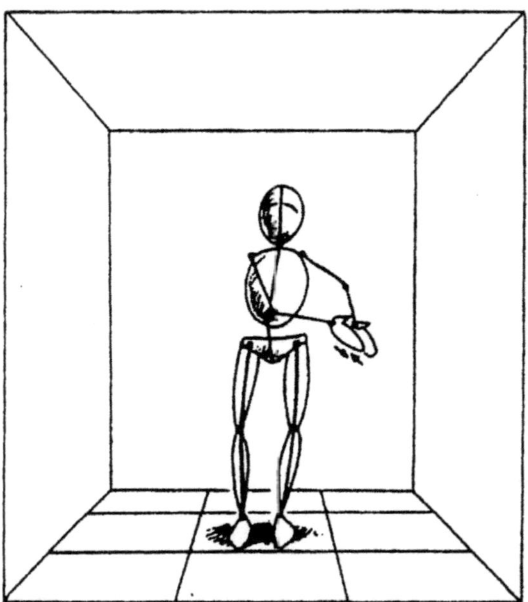

Figure 44

Aspect	from ventral
Head	
Thorax	
Arms	rubbing of palms in middle position on sagittal plane
Pelvis	
Legs	
Longitudinal axis	
Cervical vertebrae	
Shoulder	l: abduction; r: abduction
Elbow	flexion
Wrist	
Hip	
Knee	
Ankle	

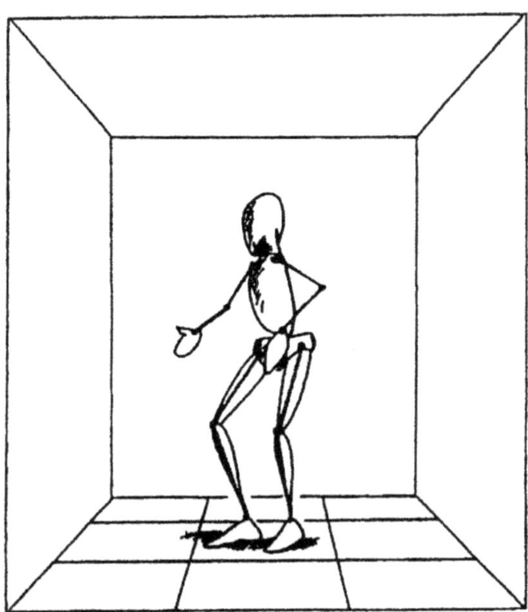

Figure 45

Aspect	from lateral left
Head	
Thorax	
Arms	
Pelvis	
Legs	
Longitudinal axis	
Cervical vertebrae	
Spinal column	rotation to the right
Shoulder	l: abduction, outward rotation; r: abduction, outward rotation
Elbow	l: flexion; r: middle position
Wrist	middle position
Hip	l: middle position; r: abduction
Knee	
Ankle	

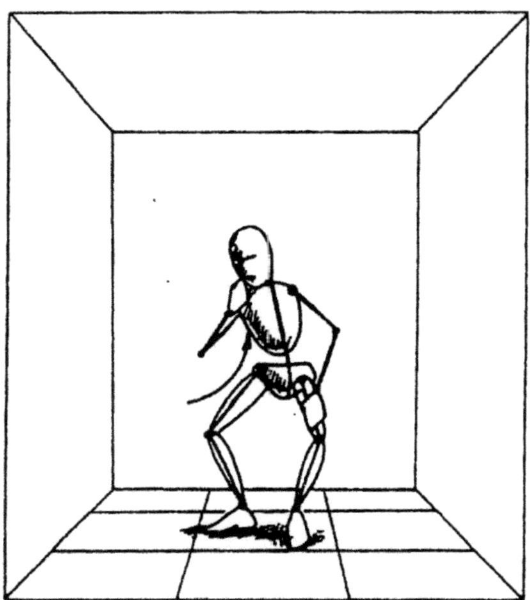

Figure 46

Aspect	from ventral
Head	
Thorax	
Arms	fingers of the right hand: flexion against the thumb
Pelvis	
Legs	
Longitudinal axis	rotation towards lateral left
Cervical vertebrae	rotation to the left
Shoulder	l: abduction; r: abduction
Elbow	r: flexion, extension (gradual, repetitive)
Wrist	r: extension, supination
Hip	
Knee	
Ankle	

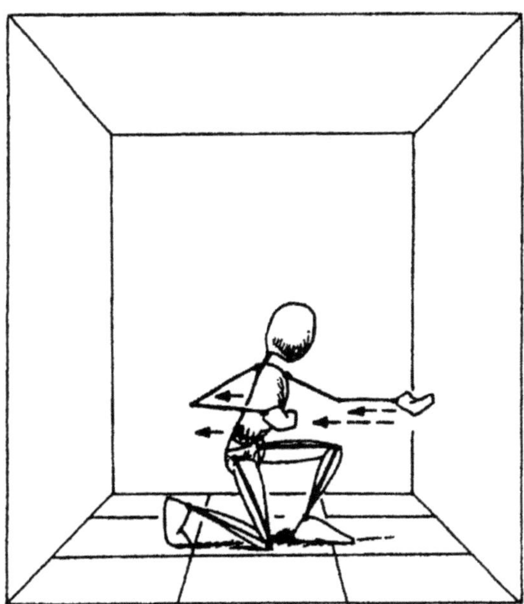

Figure 47

Aspect	from lateral right
Head	
Thorax	
Arms	l; r: make hand into fist, all fingers flexion
Pelvis	
Legs	half-kneeling (right) with extended foot
Longitudinal axis	
Cervical vertebrae	flexion
Shoulder	l: flexion; r: extension
Elbow	l: supination; r: flexion on the transversal plane
Wrist	l: supination; r: middle position
Hip	
Knee	
Ankle	

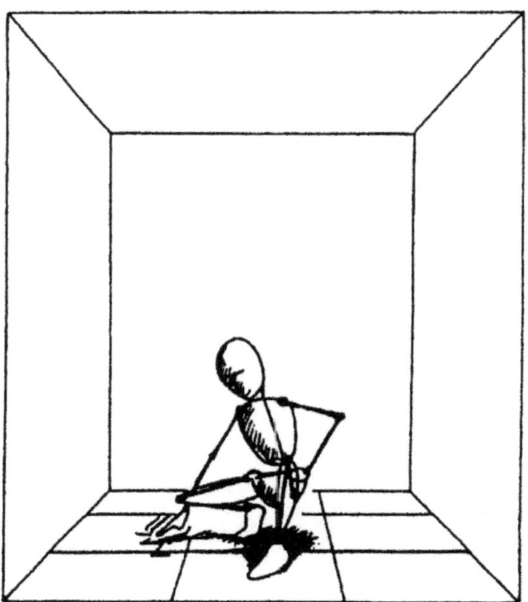

Figure 48

Aspect	from lateral left
Head	line of sight towards the floor
Thorax	
Arms	writing motion
Pelvis	
Legs	
Longitudinal axis	
Cervical vertebrae	flexion towards ventral
Shoulder	l: abduction, adduction in extension (repeated in half-circle movement)
Elbow	
Wrist	r: extension (index finger), flexion thumb (pollex), middle finger (medius), ring finger (amularius), little finger (digitus minimus)
Hip	
Knee	flexion l and r, half-crouched
Ankle	

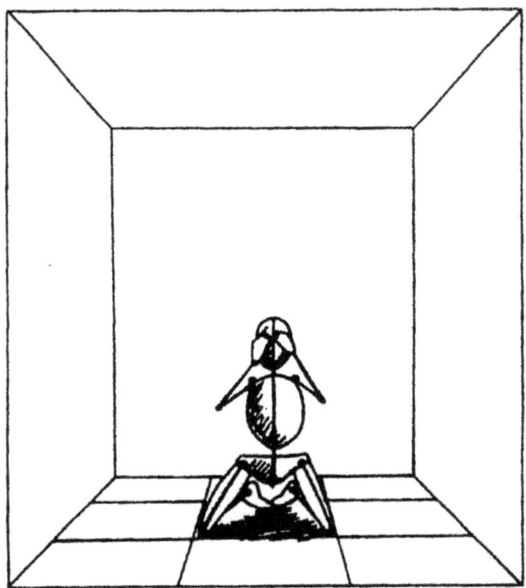

Figure 49

Aspect	from ventral
Head	
Thorax	
Arms	palms cover the eyes, fingertips touch the forehead
Pelvis	extension hips, pelvis upright
Legs	kneeling
Longitudinal axis	
Cervical vertebrae	
Shoulder	l: inward rotation, flexion; r: inward rotation, extension
Elbow	l: flexion; r: flexion
Wrist	
Hip	Extension
Knee	Flexion
Ankle	Flexion

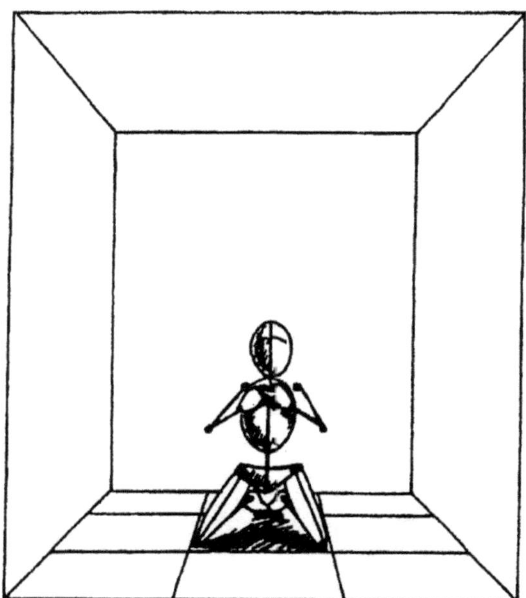

Figure 50

Aspect	from ventral
Head	
Thorax	
Arms	finger tips touch the sternum
Pelvis	
Legs	
Longitudinal axis	
Cervical vertebrae	
Shoulder	
Elbow	
Wrist	
Hip	
Knee	
Ankle	

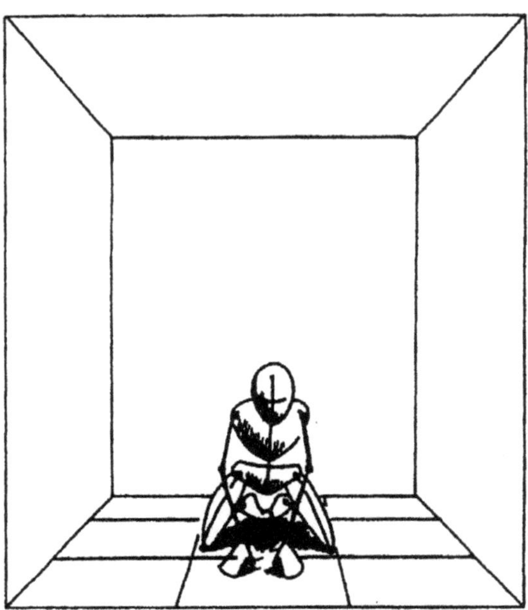

Figure 51

Aspect	from ventral
Head	
Thorax	flexion towards ventral
Arms	finger tips touch the floor in pronation with palms down
Pelvis	
Legs	kneeling
Longitudinal axis	
Cervical vertebrae	
Shoulder	l: flexion, inward rotation; r: abduction, inward rotation
Elbow	
Wrist	
Hip	Extension
Knee	Flexion
Ankle	Flexion

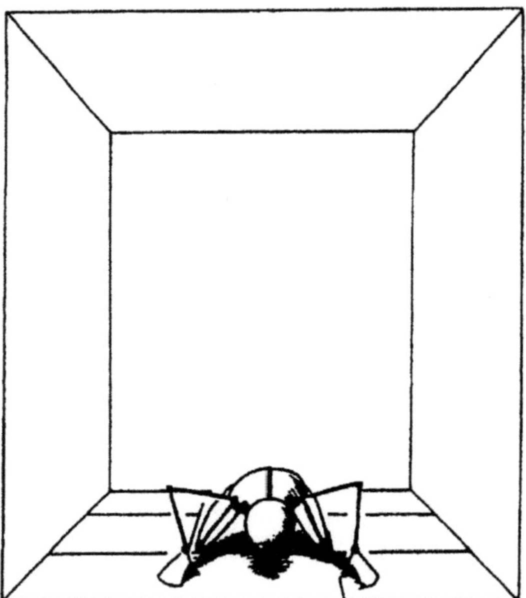

Figure 52

Aspect	from cranial
Head	
Thorax	rotation to the left, flexion
Arms	hands touch the floor in pronation with palms down
Pelvis	
Legs	
Longitudinal axis	
Cervical vertebrae	
Shoulder	l: flexion; r: flexion
Elbow	
Wrist	
Hip	
Knee	
Ankle	l: flexion; l: flexion

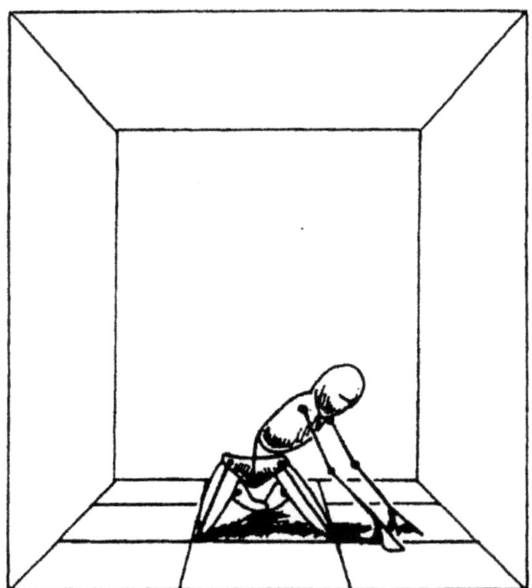

Figure 53

Aspect	
Head	
Thorax	rotation to the left, flexion
Arms	hands touch the floor in pronation with palms down
Pelvis	
Legs	
Longitudinal axis	
Cervical vertebrae	flexion towards ventral
Shoulder	l: flexion; r: flexion
Elbow	
Wrist	
Hip	
Knee	
Ankle	

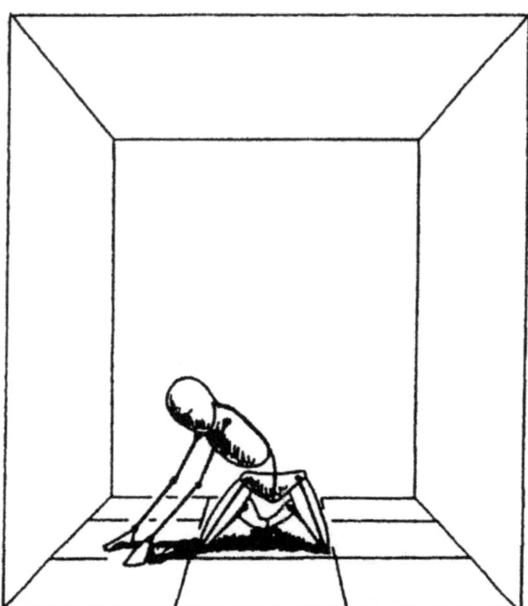

Figure 54

Aspect	
Head	
Thorax	rotation to the right, flexion
Arms	hands touch the floor in pronation with palms down
Pelvis	
Legs	
Longitudinal axis	
Cervical vertebrae	flexion towards ventral
Shoulder	l: flexion; r: flexion
Elbow	
Wrist	
Hip	
Knee	
Ankle	

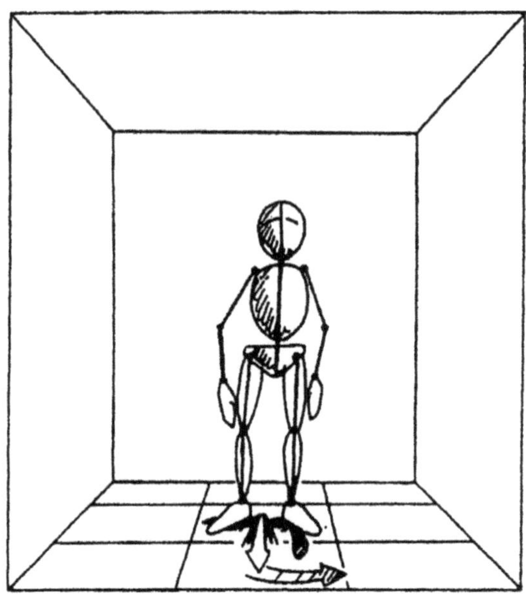

Figure 55

Aspect	
Head	
Thorax	
Arms	
Pelvis	
Legs	step to the front left with jump to the left
Longitudinal axis	
Cervical vertebrae	
Shoulder	
Elbow	
Wrist	
Hip	
Knee	
Ankle	

13. Discussion of dance data

The dance, in its entirely, is a motion continuum. It can be split into various *levels* and then further subdivided.

		D	A	N	C	E		
interval	sequence 1	interval	sequence 2	interval	sequence X	interval		
	Mo1- Mo2- Mo x		Mo1- Mo2- Mo x		Mo1- Mo2- Mo x			
S1 S2 S3 S4 S5 S6 .... Sx								
Mo = Motion unit, S = segment, position								

The highest level is that of the dance being completed. Lower levels deal with subdivided units of motion. These units are a transposition of:

a) the aforementioned acoustic (**music-rhythmic**) signals into physical-rhythmic motion (**rhythmic motion**)
b) the aforementioned acoustic (drum language) content-related signals into physical, textualised motion (**textual motion**).

Units of motion are further subdivided to achieve the lowest level or segments, which can be described using an anatomical framework. The derived positions are unachievable in 'real-time' and are thus to be accepted as 'idealised' versions of reality. The entire dance is a succession of ten sequences.

It begins and ends with an 'interval', also consisting of music and dance with rhythmic gesturing. It rounds off the previous sequence and heralds the next. Each sequence is based on a passage of text. A sequence can comprise text-based gestures or text and rhythm-based gestures which can be repeated over and over again, a feature of all the dances that I have observed. The dance is a metaphor of ten consecutive sentences which, although thematically consistent, may not be directly 'relevant' to each other. They are interdependent.

To *fully* appreciate the 'greater picture' one would have to incorporate a thorough analysis of the music and the context of the music within this dance. Whilst I can acknowledge the relationship, here is not the place to undertake such work.

The dancer translates music-rhythmic signals and drum text into dance.

	Step 1	**Step 2**	**Step 3**
Acoustic signal: rhythm of the music	Perception and decoding of the rhythmic pattern	Planning and programming of the movement with respect to the rhythmic pattern	Performing the rhythmic movement patterns
	Step 1	**Step 2**	**Step 3**
Acoustic signal: talking drum	Perception and decoding of the talking drum	Planning and programming of the movement with respect to the message of the talking drum	Performing the movement with respect to the message of the talking drum
	Step 1	**Step 2**	**Step 3**
In general:	Decoding	Encoding	Optical signal

The audience is a part of the overall experience as well. Participation takes many forms. Here too, one could undertake research into the relationships between audience and music and audience with the dance.

14.   From gesture to text

Movements relating to relevant parts of the text (numbered 1–10) and the interval (II), will now be examined.

The Adzogbo was formerly used as battle preparation for warriors. Its purpose was to:
a) physically prepare the warriors.
b) impart battle strategy and help orientate the warriors during the fight. The dancers and musicians were taught by a teacher brought in from Benin (Fon), meaning that this version of the Adzogbo is actually a re-imported version of the original.

The text as translated from Ewe

1. **"Before undertaking something, one should salute the ancestors from the west and the east, (especially those steeped in Voodoo) to ask for their blessings and to pray."**

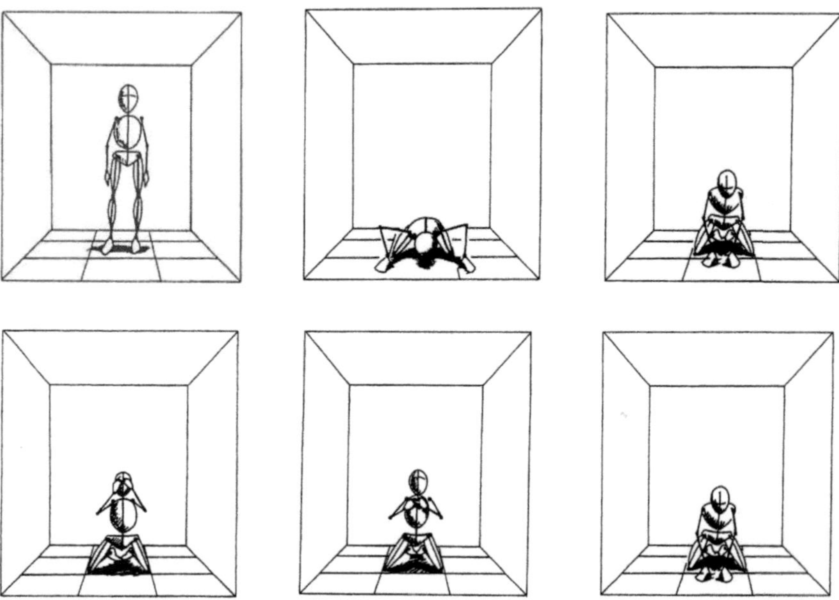

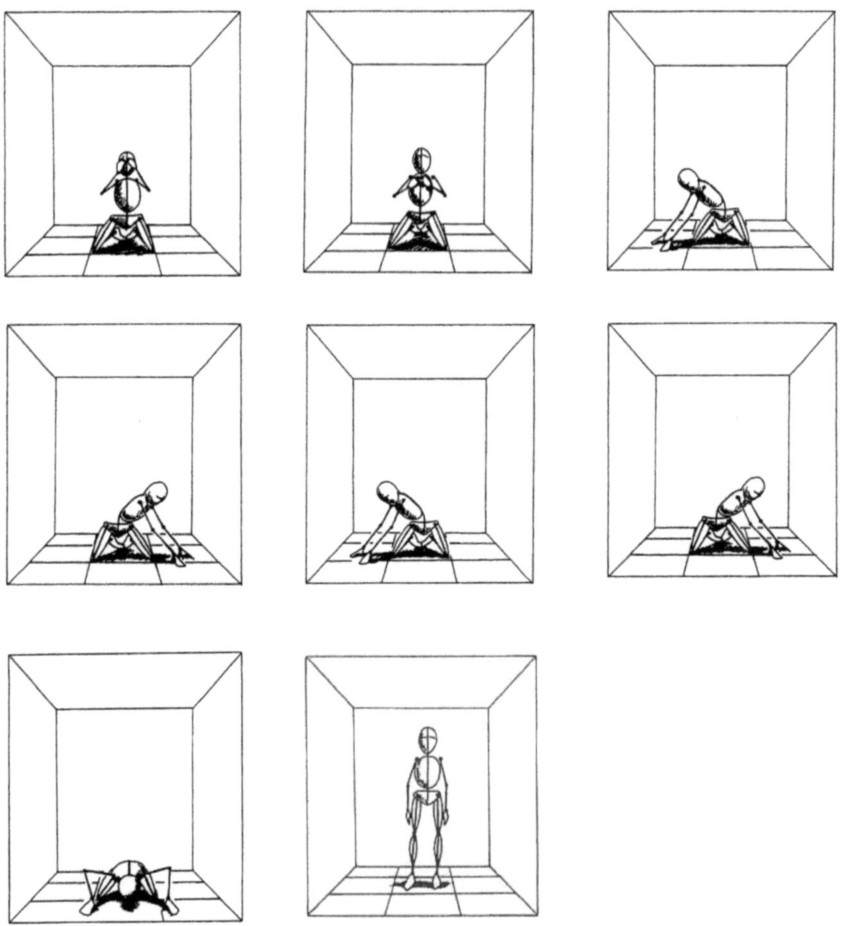

The text is primarily represented by arm, leg and head movements, and those of the upper body:

i)   arm movements refer to "salute the ancestors in the east and west". Movements left and right relate to the heavens.

ii) touching the forehead, the sternum and the floor refer to "receiving their blessing."

iii) "and pray" is symbolised by the touching of the head on the ground.

2. "Baku greets the elders and the dead."

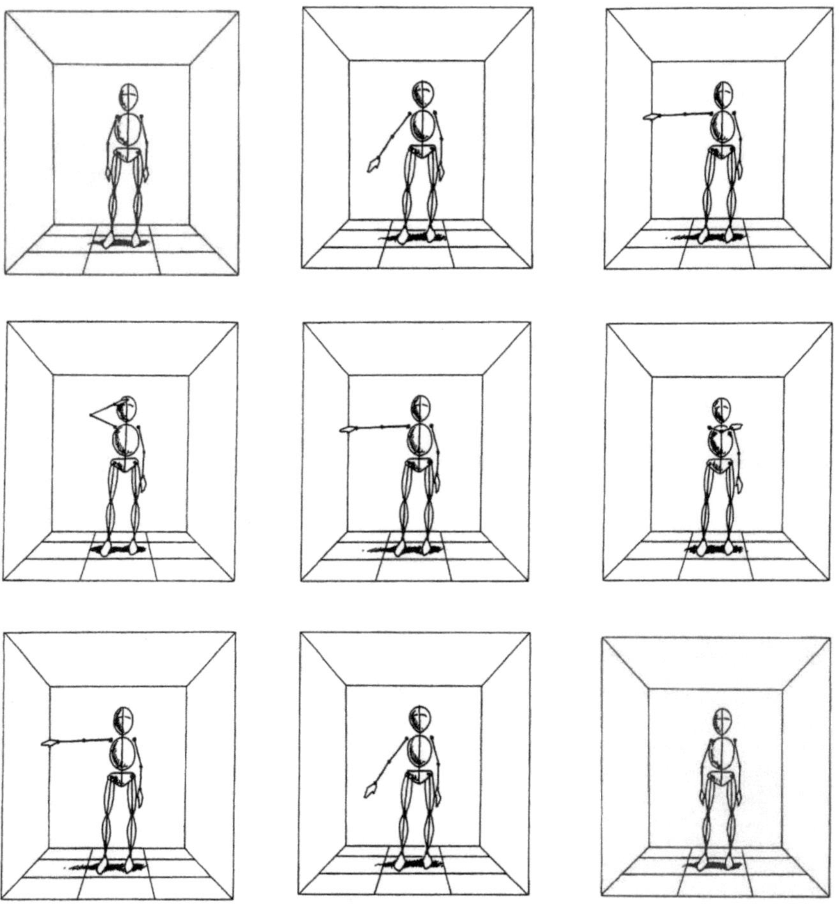

The movements are repeated once. The right arm signals the text, from the O-position to the left and right. These symbolic nine gestures of greeting could possibly have been learnt from the colonial military of the time.

3. **"Before you engage in battle, prepare yourself to receive strength from the dead and check your weapons."**

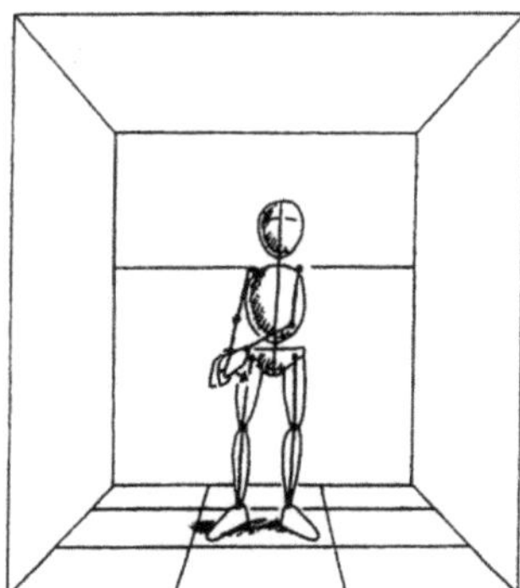

The hands represent the text, "check your weapons." One could not ascertain just how far the movements were representative of the rest of the text.

4. **"Think about that which is in front of and behind you in the field and weigh it all up."**

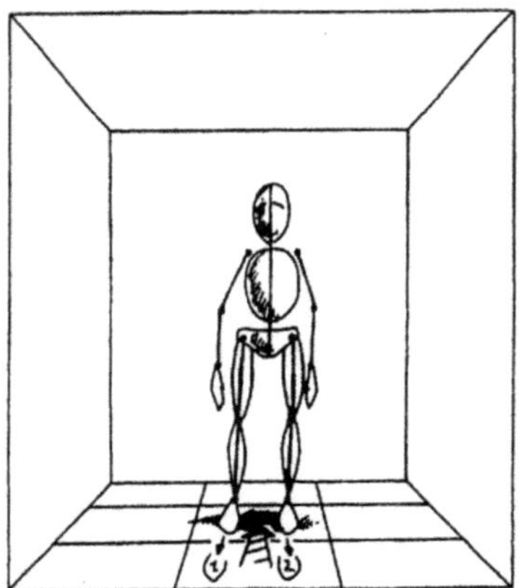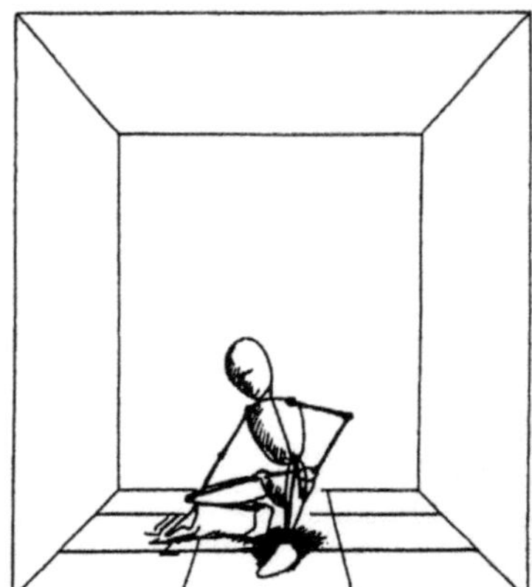

The text is represented by left and right leg and right arm movements.
i) "in front of you" is set as a step forward to the right and left; "behind you in the field" as a backward jump with both legs.
ii) "weigh it all up" is portrayed by a symbolic-metaphorical movement of the right arm. The action of 'writing' represents the text. The gesture is interesting in itself as it reveals something about the period of its origin. It could only have been devised after the introduction of writing.

5. **"If your opponent is strong, engage your strength to defeat him."**

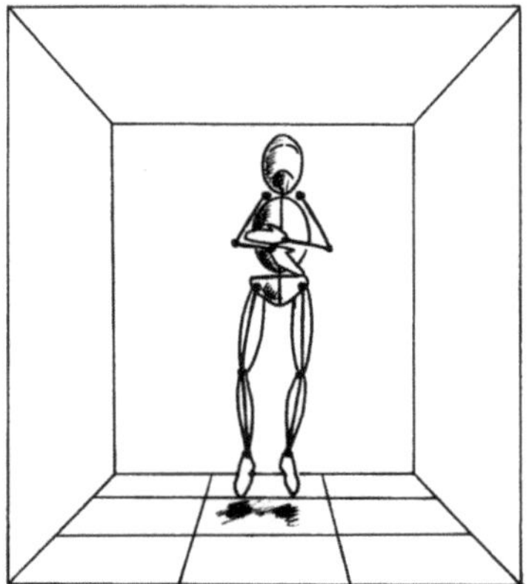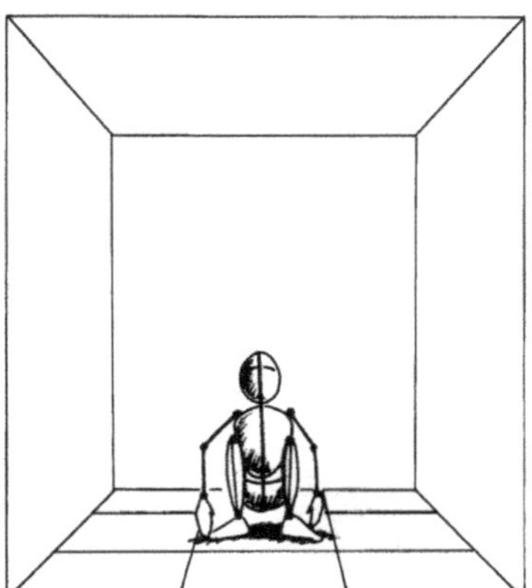

Motion direction here is both up and down and predominantly governed by the legs.
i) The jump establishes the strength of the opponent.
ii) Crouching establishes the defeat of the opponent.

These too are metaphors as:
a) by extending the body, the jump displays the body in a larger, stronger way,
b) crouching does not only show a bodily contraction (taking strength away) but also changes the spatial plane (lower).

6. **"Only together can we win; divided we fall."**

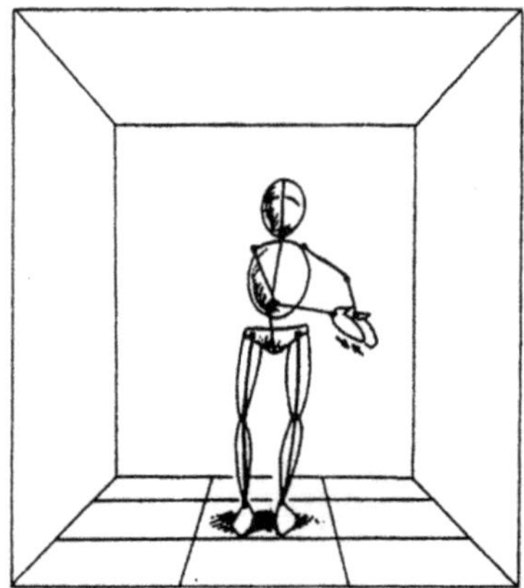 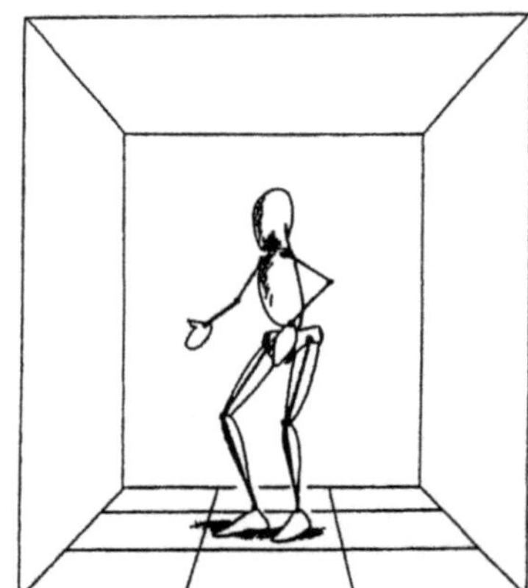

Two symbolic gestures represent the text:
i) "divided we fall", as rubbing the hands together.
ii) Shaking hands demonstrates victory through togetherness. Shaking hands
is a metaphor for togetherness. The use of such gestures, and those of 11.2
and 11.5, show a tendency discernible in dances of other cultures (the
Kpanlogo of the Ga people). Common actions are translated via the use
of symbolic gestures into a dance-context.
The translation of concrete actions (daily situations) into the abstract
(such as textual gesture in dance) constitutes a displacement of function
and meaning.

7. **"War is a battle between hippopotamus and elephant which fight over whom goes into the water and whom comes out."**

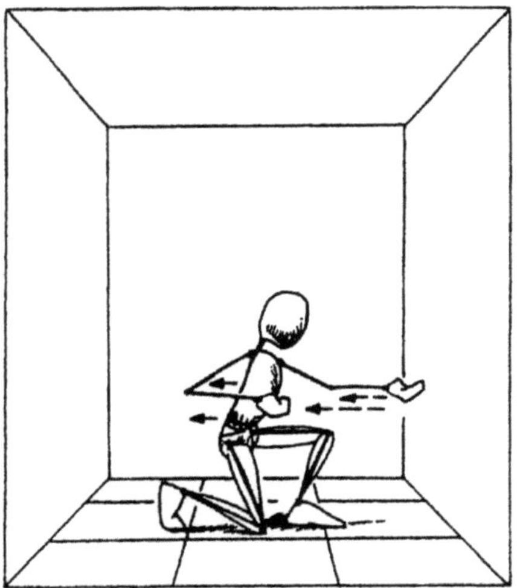

The proverb is represented via a symbolic and metaphorical gesture ('tug of war'). It is fully represented using the arms.

8. **"Only by boxing can you defend and stand up for yourself."**

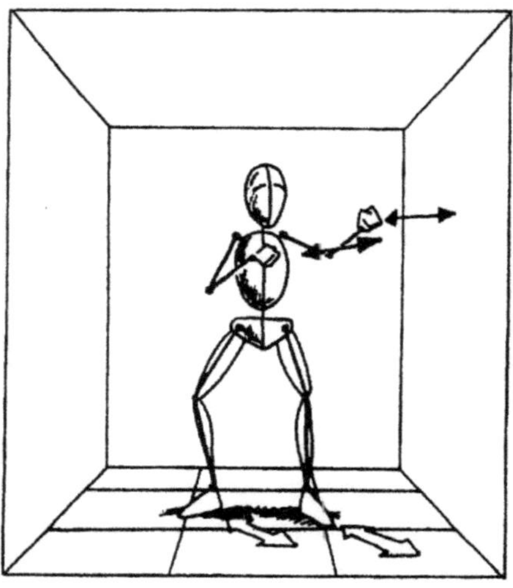

Iconic use of boxing posture.

9. "There will be times in which you get nothing to eat."

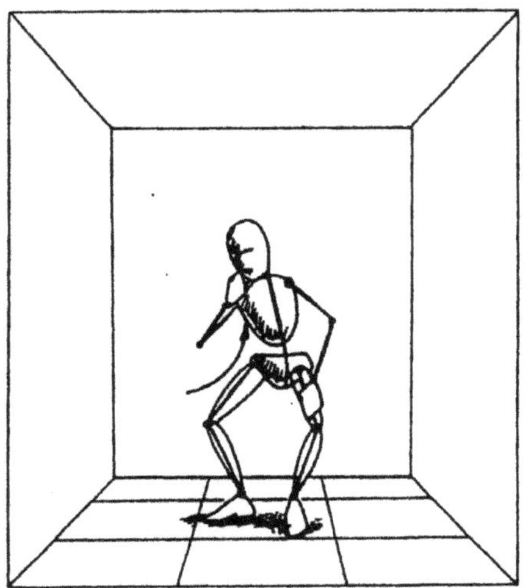

Displayed using another iconic gesture, that of raising food to one's mouth; predominantly represented by the right arm.

10. "It may be that you have to depart this world."

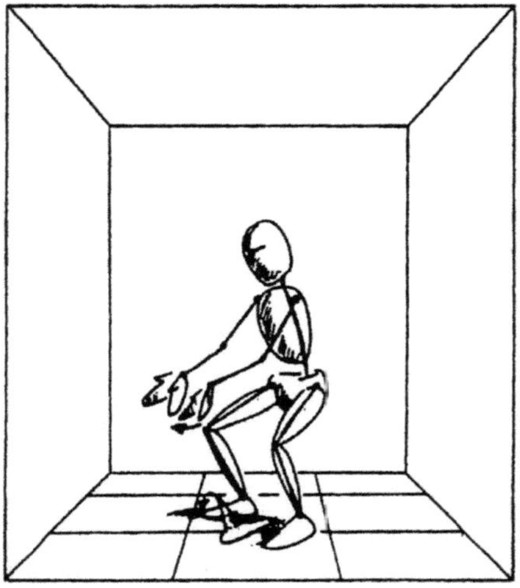

Left hand, right hand and right leg movements. Directional movement, diagonally back and to the right.

11. The Interval

An interval occurs at the beginning, the end and in between each sequence. There are no textual gestures. It is rhythmically musical (speed, breaks) by nature and uses rhythmic gesture alone. Factors such as longevity and intensity of motion are not to be examined. In the course of events the interval is repeated twelve times.

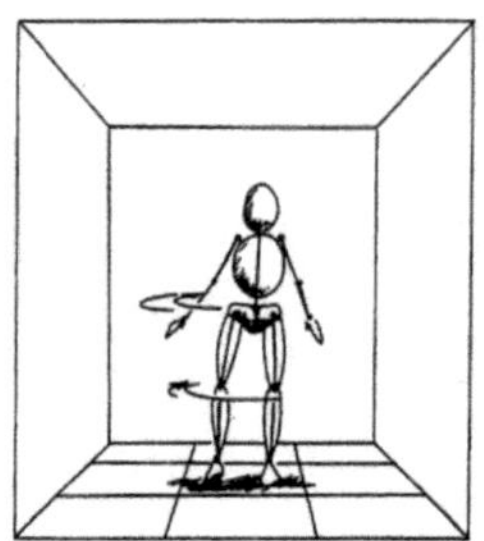 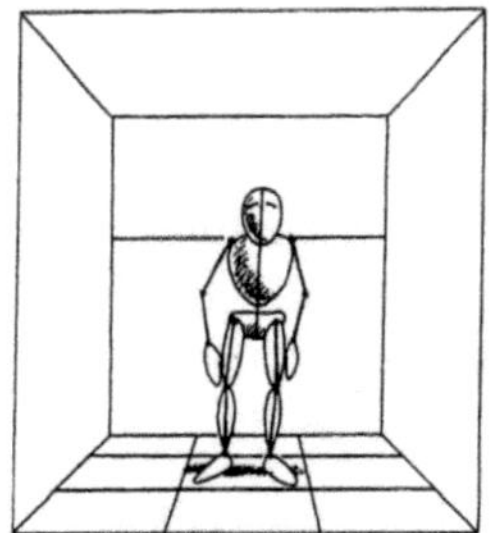

Glossary of terminology

Course of movement:	Motion during which several operators are used, during which the operator can move.
Description:	Explanation of a course of movement or a position.
Locomotion:	Human movement, from one point in space to another. Mostly leg movement.
Motion:	Voluntary, active movement of one or more operators.
Operator:	Part or section of the body bringing about movement.
Position:	Posture, placement. Here as idealised, not achievable in dance.
Dance:	Refers to a) an abstract event, b) a single dance.
Dancing:	The concrete act, deed.
Textual gesture:	Refers to the entire course of movement relating to text. Content related, meaningful.

The entire course of the Adzogbo is represented as follows:

Interval

120

1. "Before undertaking something, one should salute the ancestors from the west and the east, (especially those steeped in Voodoo) to ask for their blessings and to pray."

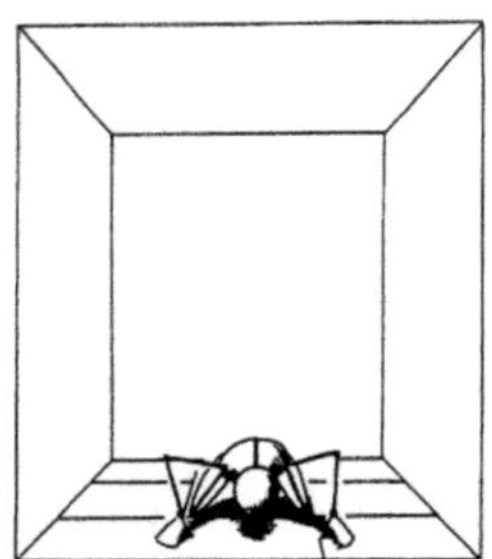 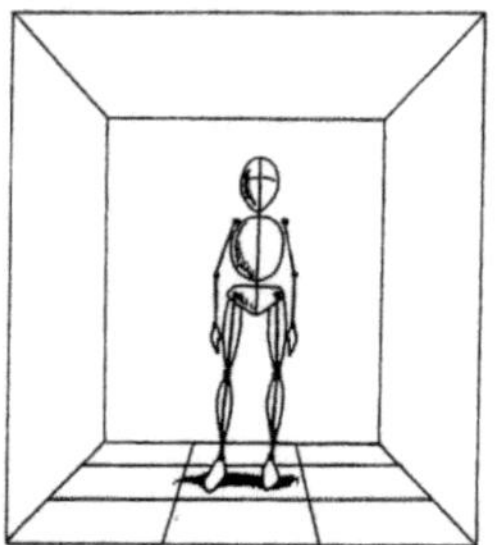

Interval

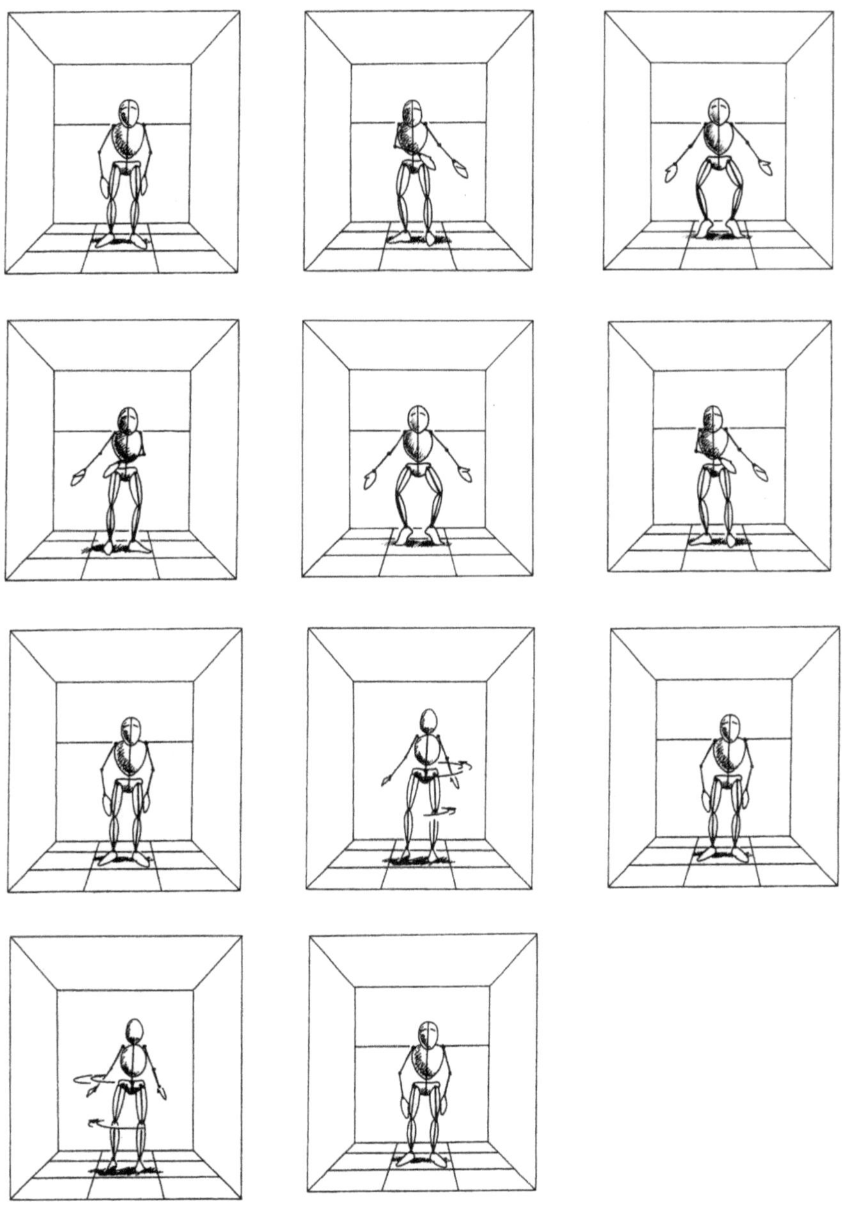

2. "Baku greets the elders and the dead."

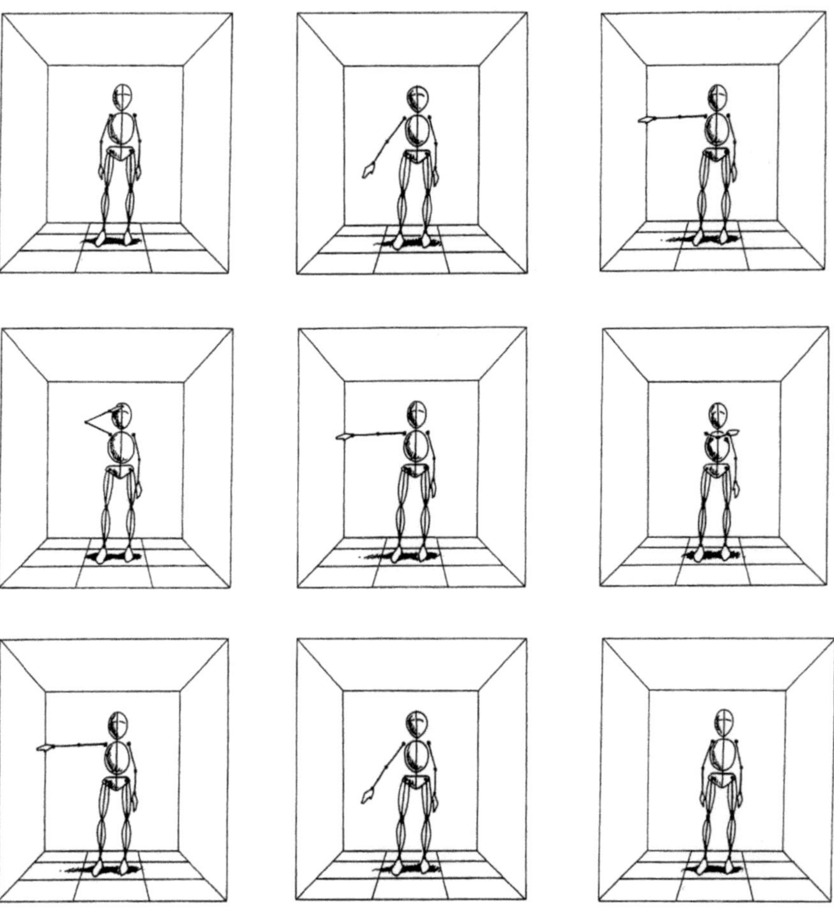

Interval

3. "Before you engage in battle, prepare yourself to receive strength from the dead and check your weapons".

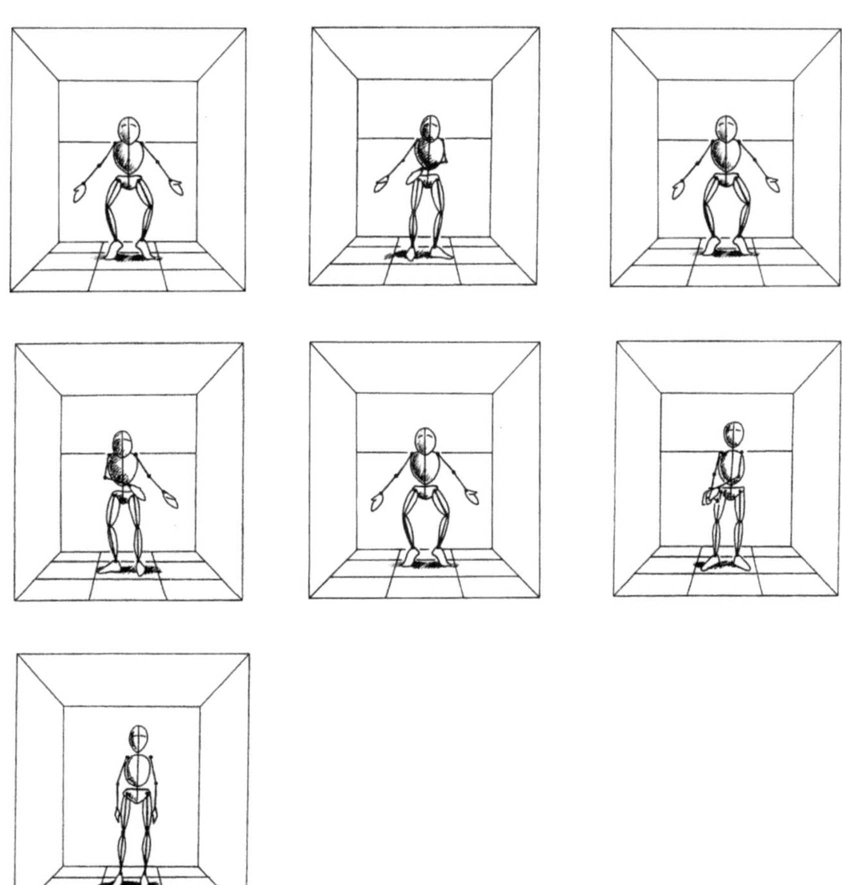

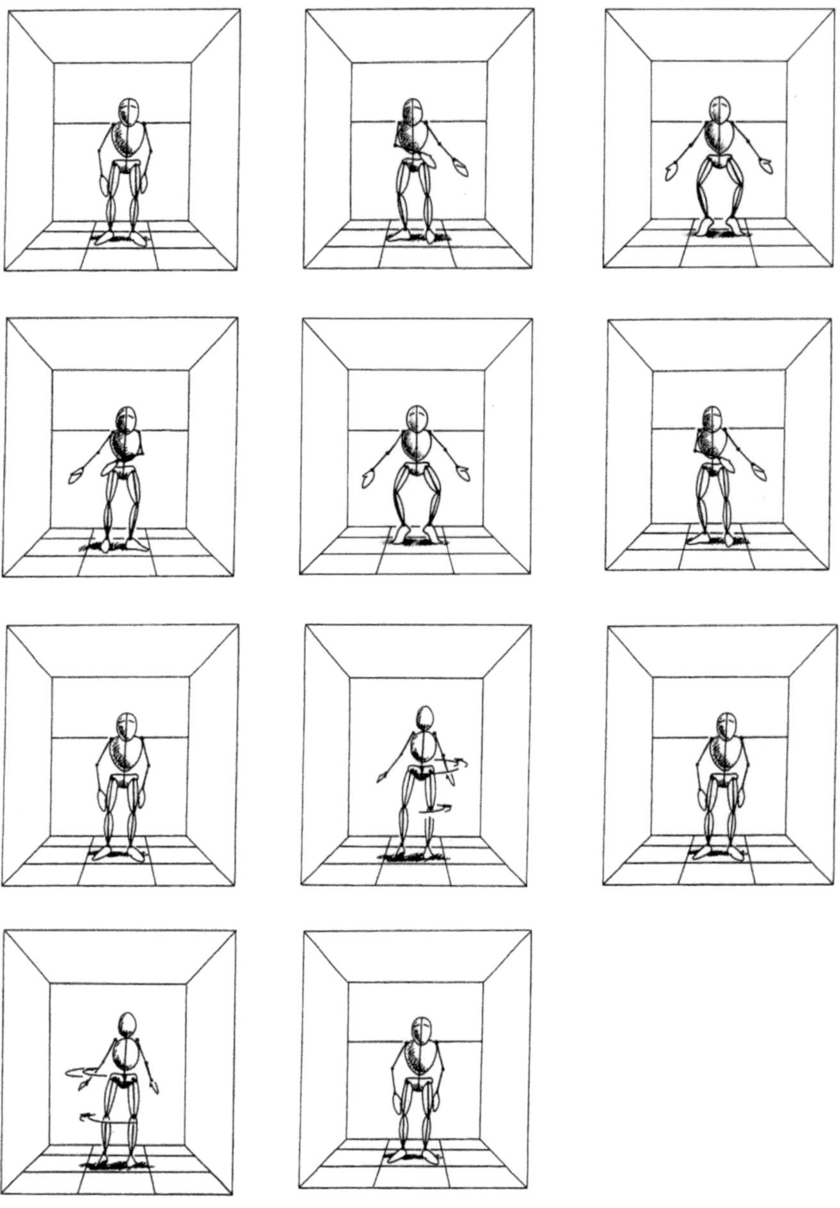

4. "Think about that which is in front of and behind you in the field and weigh it all up."

Interval

5. "If your opponent is strong, engage your strength to defeat him."

136

6. "Only together can we win; divided we fall."

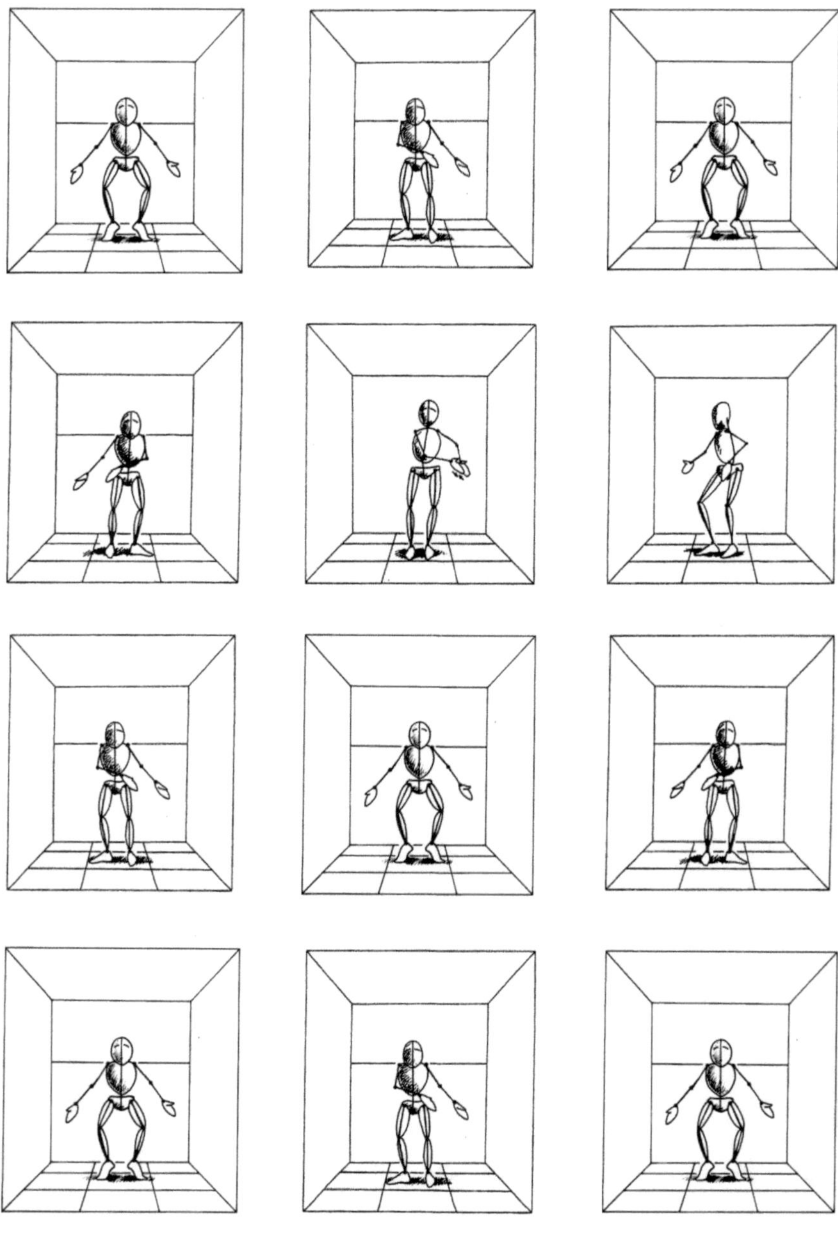

7. "War is a battle between a hippopotamus and an elephant which fight over who goes into the water and who comes out."

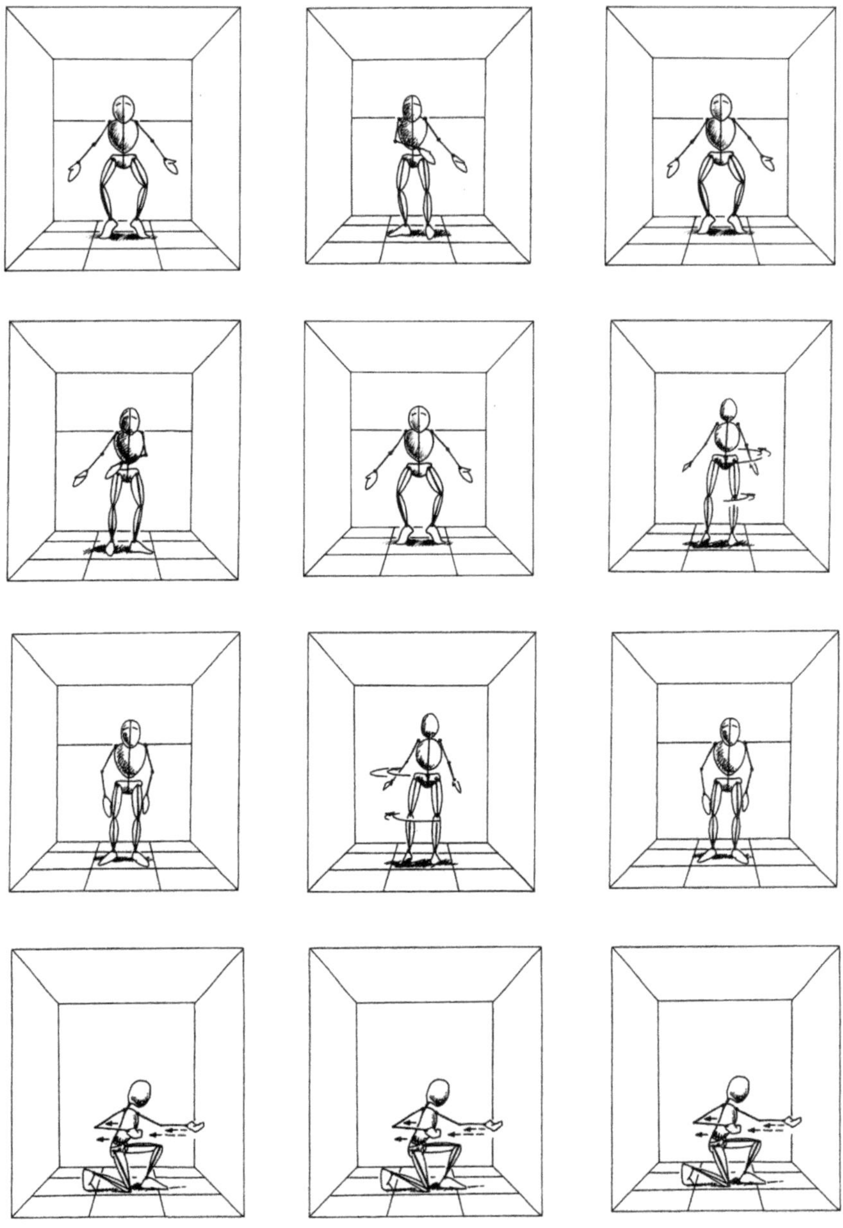

145

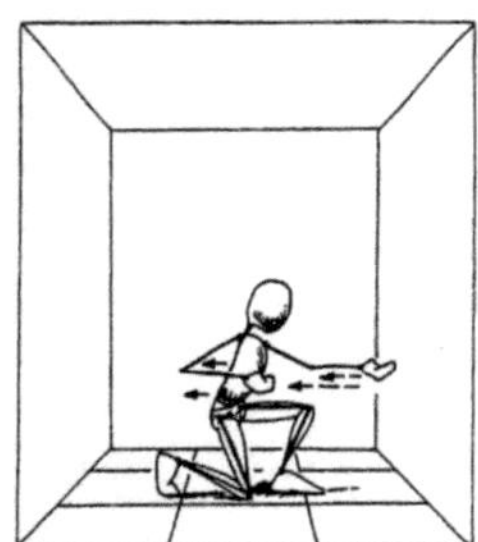 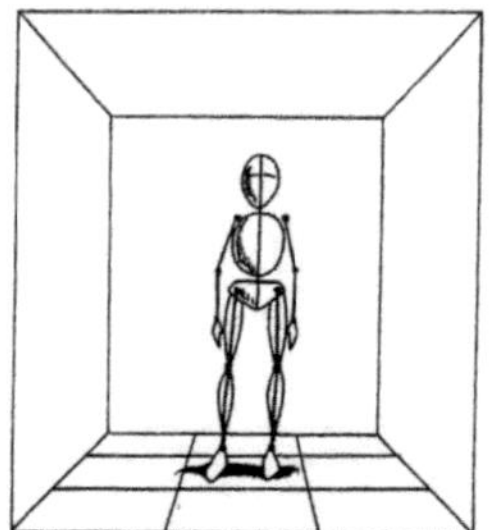

8. "Only by boxing can you defend and stand up for yourself."

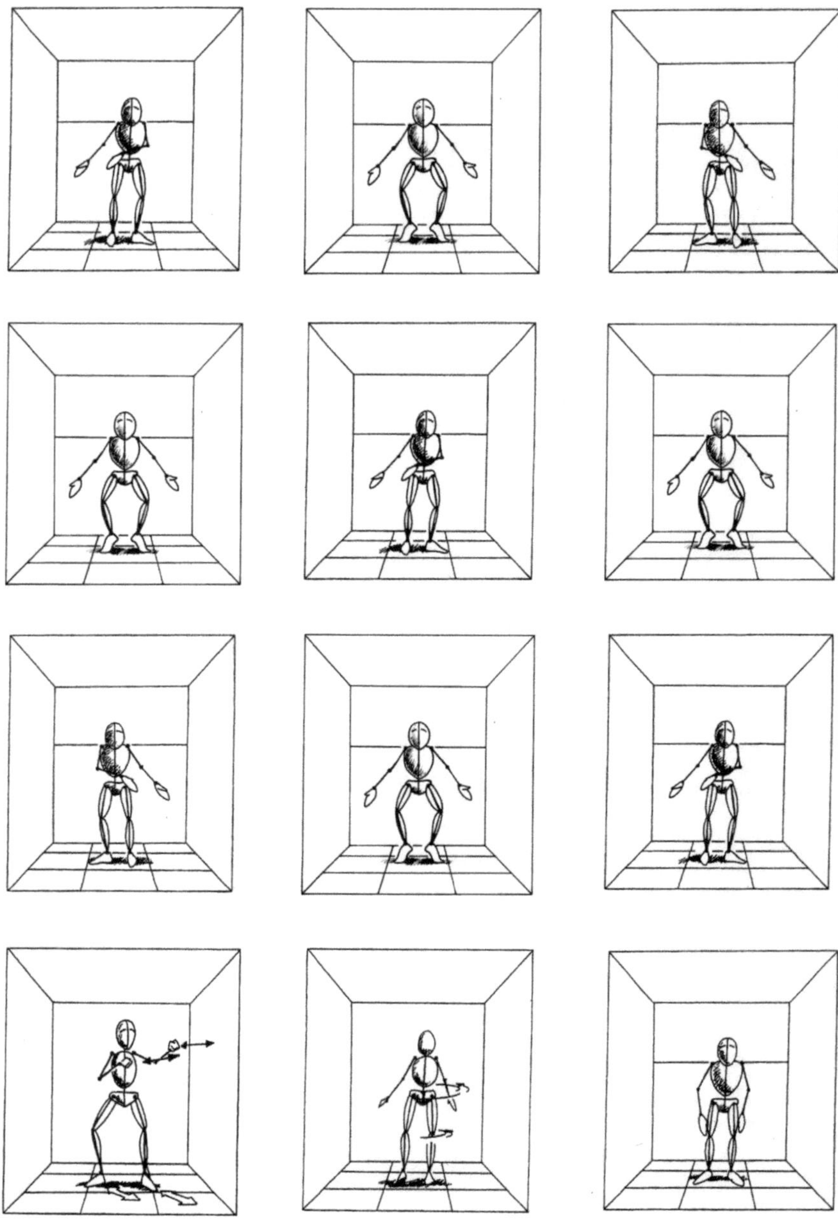

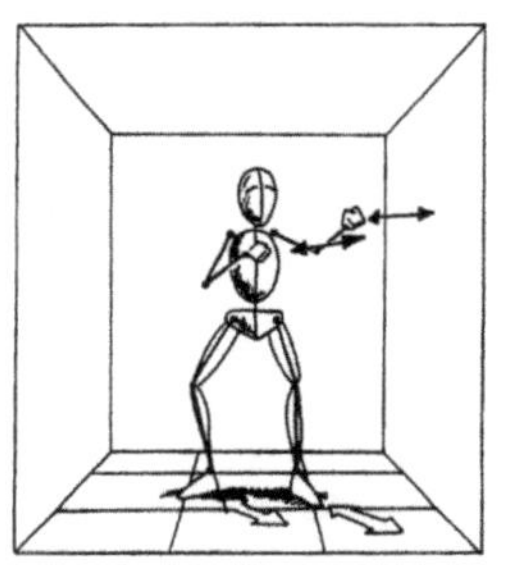 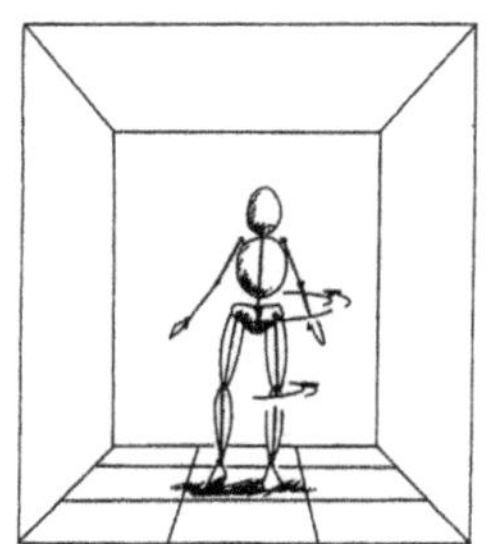 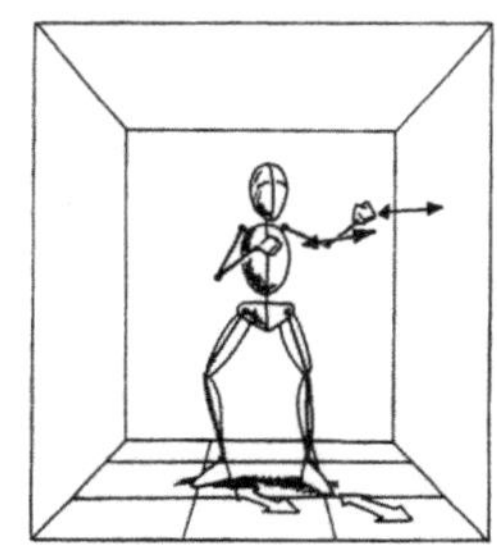

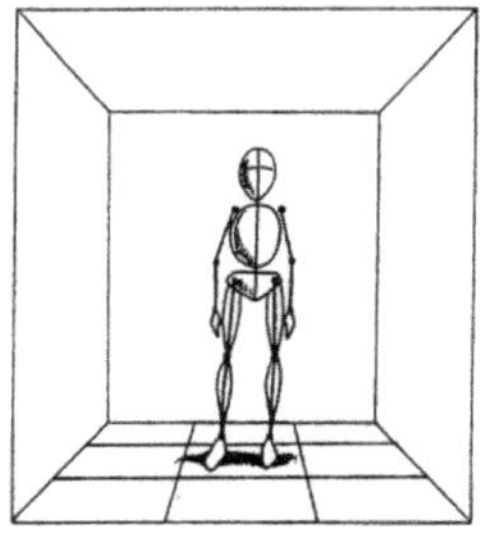

9. "There will be times in which you get nothing to eat."

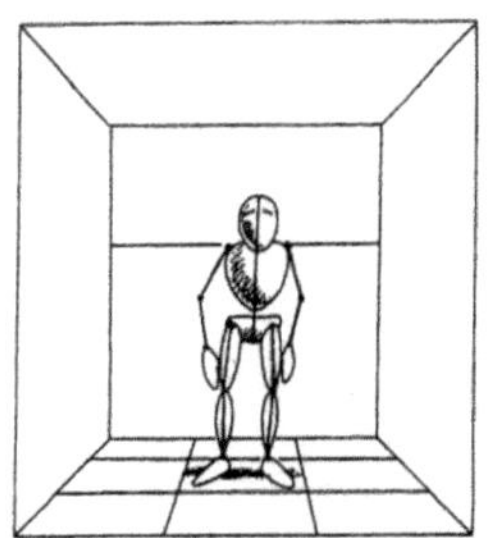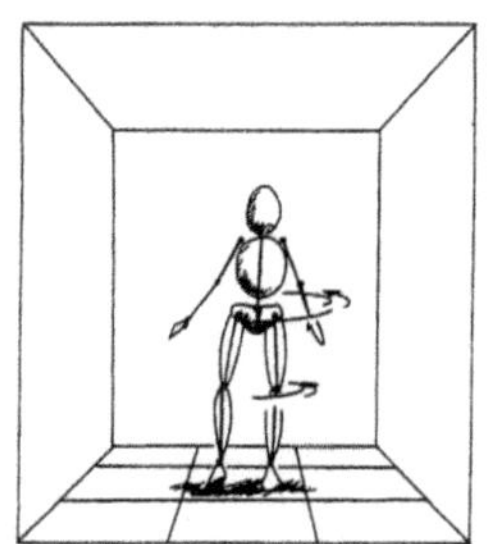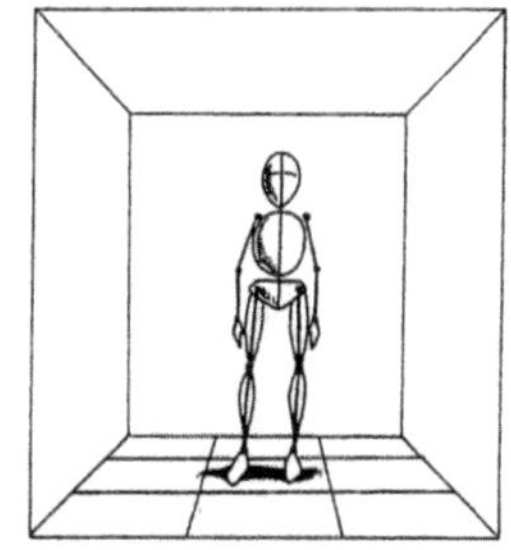

10. "It may be that you have to depart this world."

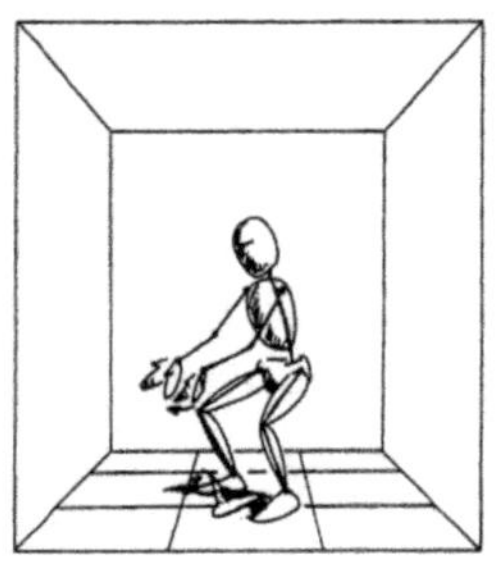
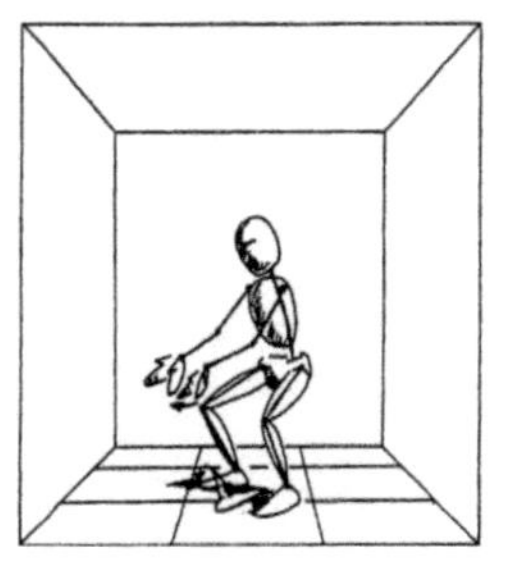
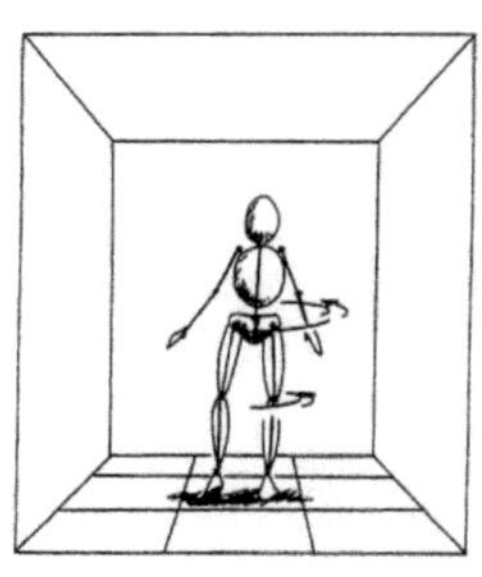
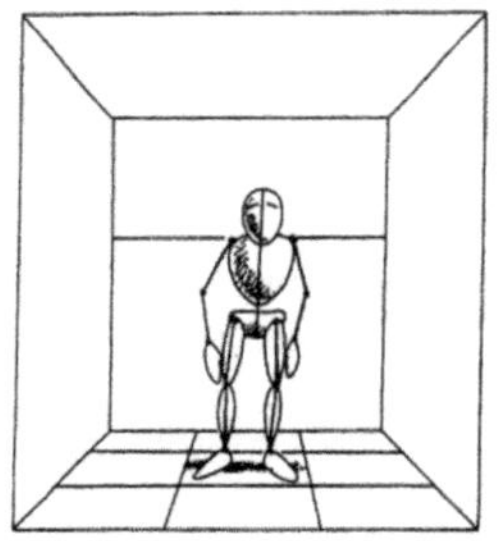
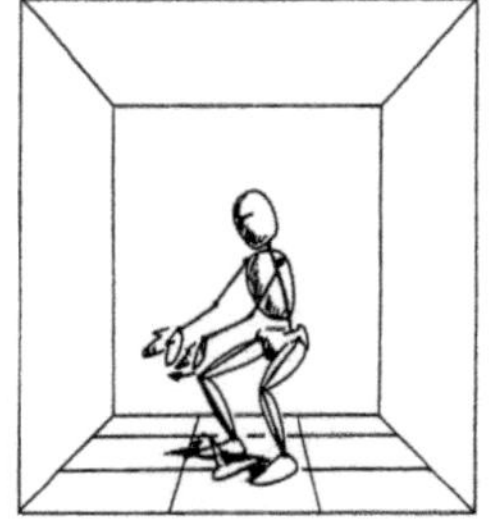
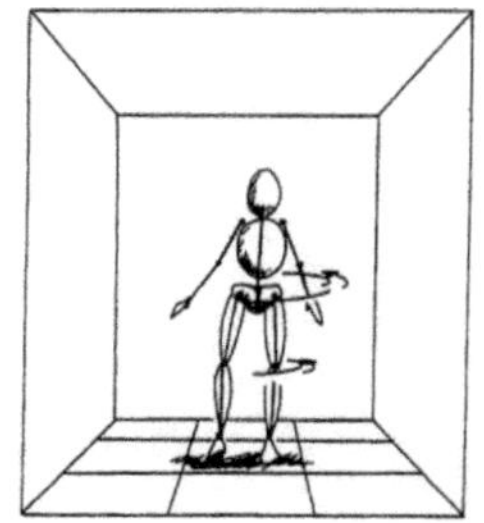
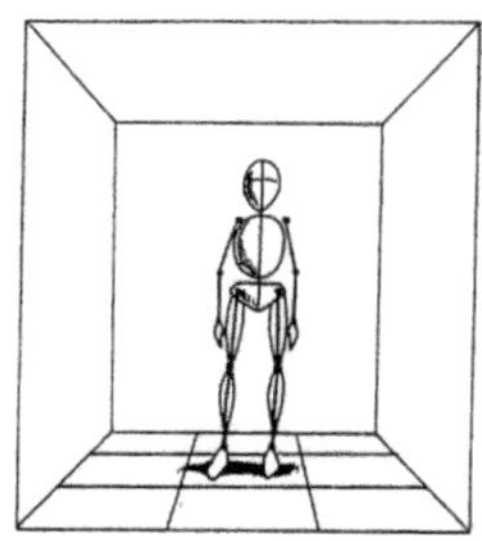

Interval

Bibliography

ABELS, B. (ed.). 2014. Zili(zo)pendwa: dance music and nostalgia in East Africa. Berlin: Verlag für Wissenschaft und Bildung.

ACKEN, S.J. v. 1929. Sport und Tanz. Saarlouis: Saarlouis Hausen.

ADAMS, M.J. 1981. "Interpretation of Masking in Black African Ritual." In: Africa Tervuren, XXVII, 2, 46–51.

ADSHEAD, J. 1981. The Study of Dance. London: o. A.

ADUAMA, E.Y. 1972. "The new Yam festival among the Ewe." In: Ghana Notes and Queries, 17, 31.

AGUILAR, M.I. 2009. The Politics of God in East Africa: Oromo Ritual and Religion. Trenton, NJ: Red Sea Press.

AKUUPA, M. 2015. National Culture in post-apartheid Namibia. Basel: Basler Afrika Bibliographien.

AMENUMEY, D.E.K. 1989. The EWE Unification Movement. A Political History. Accra: Ghana University Press.

AMOAKU, K.W. 1975. "Toward a definition of Traditional African Music: A look at the Ewe of Ghana." In: Jackson, I.V. More than Drumming. Westport: Greenwood Press.

ANING, B.A. 1972. "Tempo Change: Dance-Music Interactions in some Ghanaian Traditions." In: Research Review, Inst. of African Studies, University of Ghana, Legon, 8, 2, 41ff.

ANONYMOUS. 1966. Music of our land and our traditional dances. Nigeria Today 4th Publ. by the Federal Ministry of Information. Lagos.

ANONYMOUS. 1965. "Palaver: Dance and Music in Senegal." In: Présence Africaine, 26, 54.

AQUINO, F.R. 1953/64. Phillipine Folk Dance. Manila.

ARCHIVES of Bremen Mission, 7, 1025, 1902–1910. Depositum des Staatsarchivs Bremen.

ARGYLE, M. 1975. Bodily Communication. London: Methuchen & Co.

ARMSTRONG, D./STOKOE, W.C./WILCOX, S.E. 1995. Gesture and the nature of language. Cambridge: Cambridge University Press.

ASAMOA, A. 1971. Die gesellschaftlichen Verhältnisse der Ewe-Bevölkerung in Süd-Ost-Ghana. Berlin: Akademie-Verlag.

BAAREN, T.P. Van. 1964. Selbst die Götter tanzen: Sinn und Form des Tanzes in Kultur und Religion. Gütersloh: Gütersloher Verlags-Haus G. Mohn.

BACKMANN, E.L. 1952. Religious Dances in the Christian Church and in popular medicine. London: George Allen Ltd.

BALDISSERA, F./MICHAELS, A. 1988. Der Indische Tanz. Körpersprache in Vollendung. Köln: Dumont Buchverlag.

BALLIF, N. 1954. Les Danseurs de Dieu. Chez les pygmées de la Sangha. Paris: Hachet.

BAME, K.N. 1967. "The popular theatre in Ghana." In: Research Review, Inst. of African Studies, University of Ghana, Legon, Accra, 3, 2, 34ff.

BAME, K.N. 1991. Profiles in African Traditional Popular Culture – Consensus and Conflict. New York: Clear Type Press.

BANCROFT-HUNT, N./FORMAN, W. 1988. Totempfahl und Maskentanz. Die Indianer der pazifischen Nordwestküste. Luzern: Atlantis.

BANTA, M. 1986. To dance the Spirit: Masks of Liberia. Cambridge: Peabody Museum, Harvard University.

BARNES, H. (ed.). 2013. Arts Activism, Education, and Therapies: Transforming communities across Africa. Amsterdam: Ed. Rodopi.

BASTIAN, T. 1989. "Körperlichkeit und Selbstkontrolle." In: Universitas, 44, Vol. 1, 1, 215–224.

BAUMANN, H. 1952. "Das Tier als Alter Ego in Afrika." In: Paideuma, 5/4, 167–189.

BEATTIE, J./MIDDLETON, J. (eds.). 1969. Spirit Mediumship and Society in Africa. London: Routledge & Kegan Paul.

BEIER, U. 1964. "Agbor Dancers." In: Nigeria Magazine, 83, 241–248.

BEKKEN, K. 1989. Is there "motherese" in gesture? Ph.D. thesis, Dept. of Psychology, University of Chicago.

BENESH, R./BENESH, J. 1956. An Introduction to Benesh Dance Notation. London: Black.

BENSE, M. 1967. Semiotik. Allgemeine Theorie der Zeichen. Baden-Baden: Agis.

BENTHALL, J./POLHEMUS, T. (eds.). 1975. The Body as a Medium of Expression. London: Alan Lane.

BERGER, J. 1972. Selected essays and articles: The look of things. Harmondsworth: Penguin Books.

BERGER, R. 1984. African Dance. Afrikanischer Tanz in Vergangenheit und Zukunft. Ursprung und Diaspora. Afrika Brasilien Karibik USA. Wilhelmshaven: Heinrichshoven.

BERGER, R. 1967. "African and European Dance." In: Nigeria Magazine, 92, 92ff.

BERGHO, F. 1996. "Traditional African Dance in Context." K. Welsh-Asante (ed.), 163–182.

BERLINER, P. 1976. "Music and spirit possession at a shona bira." In: African Music. African Music Society Journal, 130ff.

BEYREUTER, E. 1978. Geschichte des Pietismus. Stuttgart: Steinkopf.

Die BIBEL. 1997. Die Bibel. Stuttgart: Verlag Katholisches Bildungswerk.

BINET, J. 1972. Société de Dance Chez les Fang du Gabon. Paris: l'Orstom.

BINKLEY, D.A. 1987. "Avatar of power: Southern Kuba Masquerade Figures in a funerary context." In: Africa, 57, 75–97.

BIRDWHISTELL, R.L. 1970. Kinesic and Context. Pennyslvania University Press, Pennsylvania.

BIRDWHISTELL, R.L. 1952. Introduction to Kinesics. Louisville.

BLACKING, J. (ed.). 1977. The Anthropology of the Body. London: Academic Press.

BLACKING, J. 1956–58. "Dance and Music in the Venda children's cognitive development." In: BN, 90, 91–112.

BLACKING, J./KEALIINOHOMOKU, J.W. (eds.). 1979. The Performing Arts. Music and Dance. Paris: Mouton.

BLATT, G./CUNNINGHAM, J. 1981. It's your move. Expressive Movement Activities for Language Arts Class. New York & London: Teachers College Press, Columbia University.

BOAS, F. 1972. The function of dance in Human Society. Brooklyn, New York.

BOEHN, M. v. 1925. Der Tanz. Berlin: Volksverband der Bücherfreunde, Wegweiser-Verlag.

BÖHME, P. 1980. Geschichte des Tanzes in Deutschland. Leipzig.

BOLINGER, D. 1965. "The atomization of meaning." In: Language, 41, 4, 555–573.

BOURGUIGNON, E. 1976. Possession. San Francisco: Chandler & Sharp.

BOURGUIGNON, E. (ed.). 1973. Religion, Altered States of Consciousness, and Social Change. Columbus: Ohio State University Press.

BRADLEY, A. (ed.). 2010. The Anthology of Rap. New Haven: Yale University Press.

BREITINGER, E. 1993. "Theater in Uganda: Animation zur Nachahmung. Unterprivilegierte können sich artikulieren." In: forschung. Mitteilungen der DFG 2/93, 14ff.

BRELSFORD, W.V. 1974. "African Dances of Northern Rhodesia." In: The occasional papers of the Rhodes-Livingstone Museum. Lusaka: University of Zambia/ Manchester: University of Manchester.

BRIGINSHAW, V.A. 1987. "Giriama and Digo Dance Styles." In: African Music, 6, 4, 144–154.

BRINSON, P. 1982. What is Dance? London.

BROCKHAUS. 1973. Enzyklopädie in zwanzig Bänden. Achtzehnter Band. Wiesbaden: Brockhaus.

BROWN, P. 1994. Die Keuschheit der Engel. Sexuelle Entsagung, Askese und Körperlichkeit im frühen Christentum. München: dtv wissenschaft.

BRUNELL, G. 1977. "Le modèle linguistique en communication non-verbale." In: Communication et Information, 2, 1, 141–149.

BRUNO, M. 1972. Masques et danses de l'Afrique noire francophone. East Lansing: Michigan State University.

BÜHLER, K. 1965. Sprachtheorie. Stuttgart: Gustav Fischer.

BUONAVENTURA, W. 1990. Die Schlange vom Nil: Frauen und Tanz im Orient. Hamburg: Rogner und Bernhard.

BUTTERWORTH, B./BEATTIE, G. 1978. "Gesture and silence as indicator of planing in speech." In: R.N. Campell/P.T. Smith (eds.): Recent advances in the psychology of language: Formal and experimental approaches, 347–360. New York: Plenum Press.

CALBRIS, G. 1990. The Semiotics of French Gestures. Bloomington; Indiana University Press.

CALENDOLI, G. 1981. Tanz, Kult, Rhythmus. Braunschweig.

CHERNOFF, J.M. 1994. Rhythmen der Gemeinschaft. Musik und Sensibiltät im Afrikanischen Leben. München: Trickster.

CHILIVUMBO, A. 1969. Some traditional Malawi dances: A preliminary account. Mimeographed.

CLARK, M./CRISP, C. 1981. The History of Dance. London: Orbis Publishing.

COHAN, S.J. 1986. Aesthetics of Dance. London

COLE, H. 1971. African Arts of Transformation. Santa Barbara.

COMSTOCK, T. 1974. New Dimensions in Dance Research: Anthropology and Dance. New York.

CONTEH-MORGAN, J. (ed.). 2004. African Drama and Performance. Bloomington: Indiana University Press.

COPELAND, R./COHEN, M. 1983. What is dance? Oxford: Oxford University Press.

COSNIER, J. 1982. "Communication et langues gestuels." In: J. Cosnier et al.: Les voies du langages: Communication verbales, gestuelles, et animales. Paris: Dunod.

COURSEY, B.G. 1968. "A new Festival among the Ewe." In: Ghana Notes & queries, 10, 18–23.

CRESWELL, R. 1968. "Le geste manuel associé au langage." In: Langages, 10, 119–127.

DAGAN, E. 1992. The Spirit's Image. The African Masking Tradition-Evolving Continuity. Montreal: Galeri Amrad African Publications.

DAGAN, E. 1977. "The Possession as a source of dance." In: Israel Dance, 20–25.

DAGAN, E. 1976. "Where are the dance sources?" In: Israel Dance, 24–25.

DARBOIS, D. 1962. African Dance: A Book of Photographs. Prague: Artia.

DAUER, A. 1969. "Zum Bewegungsverhalten afrikanischer Tänzer." In: Research Film, 6, 6.

DAUER, A. 1969. "Kinesis und Katharsis. Prolegomena zur Deutung afrikanischer Rhythmik." In: Afrika heute.

DAUER, A. 1967. "Stil und Technik im Afrikanischen Tanz." In: Afrika heute, 24, 1967.

DEBRUNNER, H.U. 1971. "AO Gelenkmessung. Neutral-0 Methode." In: Dokumentation der DGTO. Bulletin, offizielles Organ der Arbeitsgemeinschaft für Osteosynthesefragen. Tübingen.

DERTING, C. (ed.). 2005. Bob Curtis: Hohepriester des Afro Contemporary Dance. Wien: Folio.

DESCHNER, K. 1994. Das Kreuz mit der Kirche. Eine Sexualgeschichte des Christentums. München: Wilhelm Heine.

DITTMANN, A.T. et al. 1965. "Facial and bodily expression: a study of respectivity of emotional cues." In: Psychiatry, 28, 239–244.

DREWAL, H.J./THOMPSON-DREWAL, M. 1990. Gèlèdé. Art and Female Power among the Yoruba. Indiana University Press.

DURR, D. 1981. Spatial orientation and the notion of constant oppositions. In: Journal for the Anthropological Study of Human Movement. New York University, Vol. 1/4, 226–245.

EGBLEWOGBE, W.Y. 1990. "Social and Psychological Aspects of greeting among the Ewes of West Africa." In: Research Review, Institute of African Studies, University of Ghana, Legon, 6, 2, 8ff.

EGBLEWOGBE, W.Y. 1976. Games and Songs as an Aspect of Socialisation of children in Eweland. M.A. thesis, University of Ghana, Accra.

EIBL-EIBESFELD, I. 1997. Die Biologie des menschlichen Verhaltens. Grundriss des menschlichen Humanethologie. München: Piper.

EIGEN, M./WINKLER R. 1978. Das Spiel: Naturgesetze steuern den Zufall. München & Zürich: Piper.

EKMAN, P. 1988. Gesichtsausdruck und Gefühl. Innovative Psychotherapie und Humanwissenschaft, Vol. 38. Paderborn: Jungfermann.

EKMAN, P./FRIESEN, W.V. 1969. "The repertoire of non-verbal behaviour: categories, origins, usage and coding." In: Semiotica, 1, 49–98.

EMERY, L.F. 1988. Black dance. From 1619 to today. London: Princeton Book Company.

EMSHEIMER, F. 1937. "Drei Tanzgesänge der Akomba." In: Ethnos, 2, 4, 137–143.

EPSKAMP, E. 1988. "Hoe krijers minnaars werden." In: Bres, Keerpunten in mens en cultuur. Amsterdam.

EPSKAMP, C.P./de GEUS, F. 1985. "Afrikaanse dans op drift." In: Muziek en Dans, 9, 7.

ESSLIN, M. 1989. Das Zeichen des Dramas. Reinbek: rororo enzykl.

ESTREICHER, Z. 1954–55. "Chants et rhythms de la danse d'hommes Bororo." In: Bulletin de la société Neuchateloise de la géographie.

EVANS-PRITCHARD, E.E. 1929. "The Dance." In: Africa 1, 1929, 446–462.

FAIK-NZUJI, A. 1993. Die Macht des Sakralen. Mensch, Natur und Kunst in Afrika. Solothurn & Düsseldorf: Walter.

FAIRBANK, H. 1983. Thinking and Movement. A critical review of Sheet-J. article 'thinking in movement'. In: Journal of the Anthropological Study of Human Movement, 12, 4.

FAWCETT, R.P. et al. 1984. The semiotics of culture and language. Volume 2, Language and other Semiotic Systems of Culture. London & Dover: Frances Printer.

FEELEY-HARNICK, G. 1988. "Sakalava Dancing battles. Representations of Conflict in Sakalava Royal Service." In: Anthropos, 83, 65–85.

FERGUSON, E. 1931. Dancing gods: Indian ceremonials of the New Mexico and Arizona. Albuquerque: University of New Mexico Press.

FEYEREISEN, P. 1986. "Lateral differences in gesture production." In: J.-L. Nespoulos et al.: The biological foundations of gestures: Motor and semiotic aspects, 77–94.

FEYEREISEN, P. et al. 1988. "The meaning of gestures: What can be understood without speech?" In: Cahiers de Psychologie Cognitive (= European Bulletin of Cognitive Psychology), 8, 3–25.

FISCHER-LICHTE, E. 1988. Semiotik des Theaters. Band 1: Das System der theatralischen Zeichen. Tübingen: G. Narr.

FISK-TAYLOR, M. 1981. A time to dance. Symbolic Movement in Worship. Library of Congres Catalog Card, Number 67-211103. The Sharing Company.

FLESHMAN, B. (ed.).1986. Theatrical Movement: A bibliographical anthology. Metuchen: N.J. Scarecrowe Press.

FLOERKE, H. 1922. Lukian. Sämtliche Werke. Berlin: Propyläen.

FODEBA, K. 1958. "African Arts and the Stage." In: World Theatre, 7, 3.

FOSTER, S.L. 1982. Reading Dancing: Gestures towards a semiotics of dance. Dissertation California.

FRANK, R.L. 1957. "Tactile Communication." In: Genetic Psychology Monographs, 56, 209–255.

FRANKEN, M.A. 1986/87. Anyone can dance. PhD, Frankfurt.

FRISCH, K. v. 1965. Tanzsprache und Orientierung der Biene. Berlin & Heidelberg: Springer-Verlag.

FRITSCH, U. 1988. Tanz, Bewegungskultur, Gesellschaft. Verluste und Chancen symbolisch-expressiven Bewegens. Frankfurt: Afra.

FROMKIN, V., 1971. "The non-anomalous nature of anomalous utterances." In: Language, 47, 27–52.

FUSTER-DURAN, A. 1995. Untersuchungen zum McGurk-Effekt in deutschen und spanischen Stimuli. Köln: Institut für Phonetik.

GARBETT, G.K. (ed). 1969. Spirit Mediumship and Society in Africa. New York: Africana Publishing Corporation.

GARDNER, H. 1974. The shattered mind. New York: Vintage Books.

GAZZANIGA, M.S. 1970. The bisected brain. New York: Appleton-Century-Crofts.

GEBANER, P. 1969. "Dances of Cameroon." In: African Arts, 4.

GELL, A. 1970. "On Dance Structures." In: Journal of Human movement studies, 5.

GERNIG, K. (ed.). 2001. Fremde Körper: Zur Konstruktion des Anderen in europäischen Diskursen. Berlin Dahlem University Press.

GINN, V. 1990. The spirited earth. Dance, Myth and Ritual from South Asia to the South Pacific. New York: Rizzoli International Publ.

GLUCKMANN, M. 1974. "The philosphical roots of Masked Dancers in Barotseland (Western Province), Zambia." In: In Memoriam Antonio Jorge Dias I. Lisbon: Instituto de Alta Cultura, 139–159.

GÖHNER, U. 1992. Einführung in die Bewegungslehre des Sports. Sport und Unterricht, Vol. 4. Schondorf: Hoffmann.

GOLDIN-MEADOW, S./FELDMANN, H. 1977. "The development of language-like communication without a language model." In: Science, 221, 372–374.

GORER, G. 1983. Africa Dances. Middlesex: Penguin Books.

GORER, G. 1965. "The function of different dance forms in primitive African Societies." In: Boas, Franziska, 1972, 21–39.

GRAF, W. 1955. "Die Tanzschrift als wissenschaftliches Hilfsmittel." In: Mitteilungen der Anthropologischen Gesellschaft, 84/85. Wien.

GRASSI, L. 1973. "Kinesics and Paralinguistc Communication." In: Semiotica, VII, 91ff.

GRAU, A. 1983. Dreaming, Dancing, Kinship: A study of yoi, the Dance of the Tiwi and Bathust Island, North Australia. Ph.D. thesis. Belfast.

GREEN, D. 1984. "Notations of African Dance and dance." In: Dance Notation journal, New York, 2, fall, 40–51.

GREENBERG, J. 1970. The Languages of Africa. Bloomington: Mouton.

GROF, S. 1978. Topographie des Unbewussten. Stuttgart: Klett-Cotta.

GROß, U. 2001. "Tanz" In: J.E. Mabe: Das Afrika Lexikon. Wuppertal: Peter Hammer.

GROß, U. 1993. "Zum Verständnis Afrikanischer Tanzkultur." In: E. Beckers/G. Schulz (eds.): Sport – Bewegung – Kultur. Bielefeld.

GÜNTHER, H. 1969. "Grundphänomene und Grundbegriffe des afrikanischen und afroamerikanischen Tanzes." In: Beiträge zur Jazzforschung, 1. Graz.

GÜNTHER, H. 1968. "Schwarzer Tanz und weißer Traum." In: Stuttgarter Zeitung, 7.4.1968.

GÜNTHER, H. 1963. "Die Tänze Afrikas." In: Deutsche Zeitung 10./11.8.1963.

HAERTEL, K. 1991. Religiöse Tänze in Tibet und ihre Bedeutung. Diplomarbeit Deutsche Sporthochschule, Köln.

HAGEMANN, C. 1919: Spiele der Völker. Eindrücke und Studien auf einer Weltfahrt nach Afrika und Ostasien. Berlin: Schuster und Löffler.

HALIFAX, J. 1983. Schamanen. Zauberer, Medizinmänner, Heiler. Frankfurt/M.: Insel Verlag.

HALL, E.T. 1969. The Hidden Dimension. N.p.: Anchor Books.

HALL, R., 1966. "The Dance societies of the Wasakuma as seen in the Masura district." In: Tanganyika Notes and Records, I, 94–96.

HALLER, S./KREMSER, M. 1975. "Danse et thérapeutique chez les Azandé." In: Bull. of the Int. Comm. on Urgent Antropology, 17, 65–79. (Ethn. Z79).

HAMMARSTRÖM, G. 1966. Linguistische Einheiten im Rahmen der modernen Sprachwissenschaften. Berlin & Heidelberg: Springer-Verlag.

HANKS, W.F. 1991. Referential practice: Language and lived space among the Maya. Chicago: University of Chicago Press.

HANNA, J.L. 1989. "African dance frame by frame: revelation of sex role through distinctive feature analysis and comments on field research, film, and notation." In: Journal of black studies, 19, 4, 422–441.

HANNA, J.L. 1989(a). Movement in african performance. In: B. Fleshman, 561–585.

HANNA, J.L 1988. "The representation of reality of divinity in dance." In: Journal of the American Academy of Religion, 56, 2.

HANNA, J.L. 1983. The performer-audience connection. Emotion to methaphor in dance and society. Austin: University of Texas.

HANNA, J.L. 1980. To dance is human. A theory of nonverbal communication. Austin & London: University of Texas Press.

HANNA, J.L. 1979. "Toward Semantic Analysis of Movement behavior: Concepts and problems." In: Semiotica, 25, 1–2, 77–110.

HANNA, J.L. 1977. "African Dance and the warrior tradition." In: Journal of Asian and African Studies, 12, 1, 4.

HANNA, J.L. 1976. The anthropology of dance ritual: Nigeria's Ubakala nkwa die iche iche. PhD, Columbia University. Ann Arbor: University Microfilm.

HANNA, J.L. 1976(a). "The highlife: a West-African Urban Dance." In: J. van Zile: Dance in Africa, Asia and the Pacific.

HANNA, J.L. 1974. "African Dance: The Continuity of Change." In: Yearbook of International Folkmusic Council, 5.

HANNA, J.L. 1966. "The status of African Dance Studies." In: Africa, XXXVI, 303–307.

HANNA, J.L. 1965. "Africa's new traditional Dance." In: Ethnomusicology, IX, 1, 13–21.

HARPER, P. 1970. "The role of dance in Gèlèdé Ceremonies of the village of Ijio." In: Odu, (Ile-Ife), 4, 67–94.

HARPER, P. 1968. "Dance Studies." In: Africa Notes, 4, 3, 5–28.

HARTONG, C. 1982. Over Dans gesproken. Rotterdam: Donker.

HASELBACH, B. 1991. Tanz und Bildende Kunst. Stuttgart: Klett.

HAWKINS, A.M. 1991. Moving from within. New York: a cappella books.

HAYES, F.C. 1940. "Should we have a dictionary of gestures?" In: Southern Folklore Quarterly, 4, 239–245.

HEIKE, G. 1975. Einführung in die Phonetik. Unveröffentlichtes Skript. Köln.

HEIKE, G. 1969. Sprachliche Kommunikation und linguistische Analyse. Heidelberg: Carl Winter.

HEIKE, G. 1960. "Musik und Sprache" In: MOVENS, Dokumente und Analyse zur Dichtung, Bildenden Kunst, Musik, Architektur. Wiesbaden.

HEINE, B. 1968. "Afrikanische Verkehrssprachen." Köln.

HEINE, B./STOLZ, Th. 1991. Creativity and Grammaticalization. Köln & Bochum: Typescript.

HENRY, J.L. 1982. "Possible Involvement of endorphines in altered states of conciousness." In: Ethos, 10, 4, 394–408.

HERMANN, A.L. 1979. "Ritual in the Celtic world: the dance of the ancient druids." In: Dance, Research Collage. Dance Research Annual X, Cord.

HERZOG, G. 1945. "Drum-Signaling in a West-African Tribe." In: Word, 1, 218–238.

HEYER, F. (ed.). 1975. Der Pietismus in Gestalten und Wirkung. Bielefeld: Luther Verlag.

HICHENS, W. 1936. "Demon Dances in East Africa." In: Discovery, 17, 198, 185–188.

HIMMELHEBER, H. 1972. "Masken, Tänze und Musiker der Elfenbeinküste." In: Publikationen zum Wissenschaftlichen Film, Sektion Völkerkunde, Vol. 2.

HINKLEY, C. 1980. Creativity in Dance. Sydney: Alternative Publishing Co-operative Limited.

HINRICHS, C. 1971: Preußentum und Pietismus. Göttingen: Vandenhoek und Ruprecht.

HJELMSLEV, L. 1974. Prolegomena zu einer Sprachtheorie. München: Hueber.

HOCHEGGER, H. 1981–1983. Le langage des gestes rituels. Volume I–III, series II, vol. 66–68. Zaire: Edition Centre Ethnologique Bandundu.

HÖRMANN, K. 1991. Durch Tanzen zum eigenen Selbst. München: Goldmann.

HOLM, N.G. 1982. Religous Ecstasy. Based on Papers read at the Symposium on Religous Ecstasy held at Abo, Finland, on the 26th–28th of August 1981. Stockholm: Almqvist & Wiksell International.

HORTON, R. 1960. The gods as guests: An aspect of Kalabari religious life. Lagos: Magazine special publication.

HUBERT, A. 1992. Das Phänomen Tanz. Gesellschaftstheoretische Bestimmung des Wesens von Tanz. Ahrensberg: Verlag Ingrid Czwalina. Sportwissenschaft und Sportpraxis, Band 90. Hrsg. Clemens Czwalina.

HUBERT, A. 1984. "Tanz als soziale Erfahrung und individuelles Erleben." In: H. Binnewies/P. Weinberg (eds): Körpererfahrung und soziale Bedeutung, 135–149. Ahrensburg: Verlag Ingrid Czwalina.

HUBRIG, S. 2002. Afrikanischer Tanz: Zu den Möglichkeiten und Grenzen in der Deutschen Tanzpädagogik. Hamburg: Diplomica.

HUET, M. 1979. Afrikanische Tänze. Köln: Du Mont.

HUET, M./KEITA, F. 1954. Les hommes de la danse. Lausanne: Edition Claire Fontaine.

HUIZINGA, J. 1987. Homo ludens: Vom Ursprung der Kultur im Spiel. Rowohlt.

HUMPHREY, D. 1985. Die Kunst, Tänze zu machen. Wilhelmshaven: Heinrichshofen.

HUTCHISON, Y. 2013. South African Performance and the Archives of Memory. Manchester: Manchester University Press.

IGWEONU, K. 2011. Trends in twenty-first century African theatre and performance. Amsterdam: Editions Rodopi B.V.

IKEGAMI, Y. 1971. "A Stratificational Analysis of the Hand Gestures in Indian Classical Dance." In: Semiotica, 4, 365–391.

ISRAEL, P. 2014. In step with the times: Mapiko Masquerades of Mozambique. Athens & Ohio: Ohio University Press.

JACOBSON-WIDDING, A. (ed.). 1991. Body and space: symbolic models of unity and division in African cosmology and experience. Uppsala Studies in Cultural Anthropology, 16, 348ff.

JAKOBSON, R. 1970. "Motor signs for 'yes' and 'no'." In: LIS I, 91–96.

JEDREJ, M.C. 1986. "Cosmology and Symbolism on the Central Guinea Coast." In: Anthropos, 81, 4–6, 479–515.

JOHNSON, M. 1987. The Body in the mind: the bodily basis of meaning, imagination, and reason. Chicago & London: The University of Chicago Press.

JOHNSTON, Th.F. 1989. "The integrative role of dance in Shangana-Tsonga Social Institutions." In: L.Y. Overby/J.H. Humphrey (eds.): Dance – Current Selected Research, Vol. 1. New York: AMS Press, Inc.

JONES, A.M. 1964. Africa and Indonesia. Leiden: E.J. Brill.

JOURARD, S.M. 1966. "An exploratory study of body accessibility." In: British Journal of Social and Clinical Psychology, 5, 222–231.

JOURARD, S.M./RUBIN, J.E. 1968. "Self-disclosure and touching: A study of two modes of interpersonal encounter and their interrelation." In: Journal of Humanistic Psychology, 8, 39–48.

KAEPPLER, A. 1978. "Dance in Anthropological Perspective." In: Annual Review of Anthropology, 7.

the Kalela dance. 1956. Manchester University Press, for the Rhodes Livingstone Institute, Paper N 27.

KAMPER, D./RITTER, V. (eds.). 1972. Zur Geschichte des Körpers. Perspektiven einer Anthropologie. München & Wien: Carl Hauser Verlag.

KASFIR, S. 1988. West African Masks and Cultural Systems. Tervuren: Musée Royal de l'Afrique centrale.

KAUFFMAN, L.E. 1971. "Tacesics, the Study of Touch: A Model for Proxemic Analysis." In: Semiotica, IV, 149ff.

KEALIINOHOMOKU, J.W. 1980. "An anthropologist looks at ballet as a form of ethnic dance." In: Journal for the Anthropological Study of Human Movement, 1, 2, 83–97 (first imprinted in: Impulse, 1969).

KEALIINOHOMOKU, J.W. 1977. "You dance what you wear, and you wear your cultural values." In: J. Cordwell/R. Schwarz (eds.): The fabrics of culture. Paris: Mouton.

KEDJANYI, J. 1972. "Masquerade Societies in Ghana." In: Research Review, Dept. of African Studies, University of Ghana, Legon, 8, 2, 51ff.

KENDALL, L. 1985. Shamans, housewives, and other restless spirits: Women in Korean ritual life. Honolulu: University of Hawai Press.

KENDON, A. 1988. "How gestures can become like words." In: F. Poyatos: Cross-cultural perspectives in nonverbal communication. Toronto: Hogrefe.

KENDON, A. 1982. "The Study of Gesture: Some Observations on its History." In: Semiotic Inquiry, Vol. 2, 1982, 1, 45ff.

KENDON, A. 1982(a). "The study of gesture: Some remarks on its history." In: Semiotic Inquiry, 2, 45–62.

KENDON, A. 1981. "Geography of gesture." In: Semiotica, 37, 129–163.

KENDON, A. 1972. "Some relationships between body motion and speech." In: A. Siegman/B. Pope (eds.): Studies in dyadic communication, 207–227. The Hague: Mouton.

KEY, F. 1980. The Study of Dance. London.

KEY, T. 1980. African Culture.

KLEIN, G. 1984. Frauen, Körper, Tanz. Eine Zivilisationsgeschichte des Tanzes. München: Heyne.

KLEIN-VOGELBACH, S. 1993. Funktionelle Bewegungslehre. Berlin: Springer.

KLEIN-VOGELBACH, S. 1989. Functional Kinetics. Observing, Analyzing and Teaching Human Movement. Berlin: Springer.

KNUFF, J./SCHMITZ, H.W. 1980. Ritualisierte Kommunikation und Sozialstruktur. Hamburg: Buske. IKP-Forschungsberichte Reihe I, 72.

KNUST, A. 1979. A Dictionary of Kinetography Laban. Vol.1, 2. Plymouth.

KOECHLIN, B. 1968. "Techniques corporelles et leurs notation symboloque." In: Langages, 10, 36–47.

KÖHLER, O. 1989. Die Welt der Kxoé-Buschleute im südlichen Afrika. Band I. Berlin: Dietrich Reimer.

KOHNO, M. 1982. "The effect of kinesic information on listening." In: The Bulletin, The Phonetic Society of Japan, 170, July, 18–20.

KRAUS, R./CHAPMAN-HILSENDAGER, S./DIXON, B. 1991. History of the dance in art and education. Englewood Cliffs, New Jersey: Prentice Hall.

KRIGE, E.J. 1950. The social system of the Zulus. Pietermaritzburg: Shuter & Shooter.

KRISTEVA, J. 1969. "Le geste, pratique on communicatio." In: Langages, 10, 48–64.

KUBIK, G. 1988. Zum Verstehen afrikanischer Musik. Leipzig: Reclam.

KUBIK, G., 1983. "Verstehen in afrikanischen Musikkulturen. In: A. Simon (ed.): "Musik in Afrika." Berlin: Museum für Völkerkunde, 313–326.

KUBIK, G. 1983(a). Kognitive Grundlagen afrikanischer Musik. In: A. Simon (ed.): "Musik in Afrika." Berlin: Museum für Völkerkunde, 327–400.

KUGLER-KRUSE, M. 1988. Die Entwicklung visueller Zeichensysteme. Von der Geste zur Gebärdensprache. (= Bochumer Beiträge zur Semiotik, 20). Bochum: Studienverlag Brockmeyer.

KURATH, G. 1960. "Panorama of Dance Ethnology." In: Current Anthropology, 1.

KUTTER, J. 1958. Leben und Werk Martin Luthers.

LABAN, R. v. 1989. Choreutik. Bern & Stuttgart: Haupt.

LABAN, R. v. 1988: Die Kunst der Bewegung. Wilhelmhaven: Nötzel.

LABOURET, H./TRAVÉLÉ, M. 1928. "Le théatre Mandingue (Soudan Francais)." In: Afrika, 1, 73–97.

LADZEKPO, S. K./PANTALEONI, H. 1970. "Takada Drumming." In: African Music, 3, 6ff.

LAMBO, T.A. 1965. "The place of the arts in the emotional life of the African." In: AMSAC Newsletter, 7, 4, 1–6.

La MERI. 1941. Indian Dance. London.

LANGE, R. 1975. The nature of dance. An anthropological perspective. London: McDonald & Evans Ltd.

LANGER, S.K. 1957. Problems of Art. New York: Scribner's.

LEE, R.B. 1967. Trance cure of the !Kung bushmen. In: Natural History, 76(a), 31–37.

LEE, R.B./KATZ, R. "The Sociology of !Kung Bushman Dance Performances." In: R. Price: Trance and Possession States. (R.M. Bucke Memorial Society, 4–6-March, 1966, 1968).

LEWANDOWSKI, T. 1980. Linguistisches Wörterbuch. Heidelberg: Quelle und Meyer.

LEWIS, I.M. 1989. Ecstatic Religion. A study of Shamanism and Spirit Possession. London & New York: Routledge.

LINDENFELD, J. 1971. Verbal and Non-Verbal Elements in Discourse. In: Semiotica, III, 1971, 223ff.

LOCK, A. 1978. Action, Gesture, and symbol: The emergency of language. London: Academic Press.

LORELLE, Y. 1974. L'expression corporelle. Du mime sacre au mime de theatre. Paris: Renaissance du Livre.

LORELLE, Y. 1964. Trente mille ans d'art du geste: de la magie à la pantomime religieuse et profane. Théâtre Paris.

LOTH, H. 1988. Audienzen auf dem schwarzen Kontinent. Afrika in der Reiseliteratur des 18. und 19. Jahrhunderts. Berlin: Union Verlag.

LOUTZAKI, I. 1984. Dance and Society. Dissertation, Belfast.

LUKAS, G. 1964. "Über die Stellung A.H. Franckes zum Körper und seiner Übung." In: August Hermann Francke. Festreden und Kolloquium über den Bildungs- und Erziehungsgedanken bei August Hermann Francke aus Anlaß der 300. Wiederkehr seines Geburtstages – 22. März 1963 –. Halle-Wittenberg.

LUKIAN. 1922. Sämtliche Werke. Band 4. Berlin: Propyläen Verlag.

LUTHER, M. 1525. "Die Fastenpostille." In: M. Luther 1927: Martin Luthers Werke. Kritische Gesamtausgabe. 17. Band. Zweite Abteilung. Weimar: Hermann Böhlaus Nachfolger.

LYNN, M. 1995. "Symbolism and Embodiment in Six Haitian Dances." In: Journal of the Anthropological Study of Human Movement, 8, 3, 93–113.

MACKAY, M. 1957. "The Atilogwu Dance." In: African Music, 1, 20ff.

MAHLER, M. 1989. Kreativer Tanz. Bern, Zyglotte.

MARSHALL, L. 1962. "The Medicine Dance of the !Kung Bushmen." In: Africa, 39, 221–252.

MARTIN, G.M. 1992. "Körperbild und Leib Christi." In: Evangelische Theologie, 52, 5, 402–413.

McNEILL, D. 1992. Hand and mind. What gestures reveal about thought. Chicago: University of Chicago Press.

McNEILL, D. 1985. "So you think gestures are nonverbal?" In: Psychological Review 92, 350–371.

MEYER, F. 1985. Milan Sládek. Pantomimentheater. Köln: Bund.

MEYER, P. 1981. Kunst und Religion der Lobi. Zürich: Museum Rietberg.

MIDDLETON, J. 1985. "The dance among the Lugbara of Uganda." In: P. Spencer (ed.): Society and the Dance: The Social Anthropology of Process and Performance, 140–164.

MITCHELL, J.C. 1956. The Kalela Dance. Manchester University Press for the Rhodes Livingstone Institute. Paper Nr. 27.

MODUM, E.P. 1979. "Gods as guests: Music and festivals in African traditional societies." In: Présence Africaine, 110, 86–110.

di MPASI LONDI, B. 1980. "Befreiung des Körperausdrucks in der afrikanischen Liturgie." In: Concilium, 16, 1, 114–120.

MURDOCK, G.P. 1959. Africa: it's peoples and their culture history. New York: McGraw Hill.

MURRAY, J. (ed.). 1981. Cultural Atlas of Africa. Oxford: Phaidon Press.

NAPIER, J. 1980. Hands. New York: Pantheon Books.

NELLE, A. Aufbruch vom Götterberg. Erlebnisbericht von der Evangelisations-Bewegung in Togo. Stuttgart: Ev. Missionsverlag.

NESS, S.A. 1987. The 'Sinulog' Dancing of Cebu City, Philippines: A Semeiotic Analysis. Ann Arbor: UMI Dissertation Information Service.

NETTL, P. 1962. tanzundtanzmusik. Freiburg, Breisgau: Herder.

NICHOLLS, R.W. 1985. "Music and dance guilds in Igede." In: I. Jackson: More than drumming. Westport: Greenwood Press.

NIEMÖLLER, K. W. et al.. 1995. "Lux Oriente." Begegnungen der Kulturen in der Musikforschung. Festschrift Robert Günther zum 65. Geburtstag. Kassel: Gustav Bosse.

NITSCHKE, A. 1989. Körper in Bewegung. Gesten, Tänze und Räume im Wandel der Geschichte. Stuttgart: Kreuz Verlag.

NITSCHKE, A. 1987. Bewegungen in Mittelalter und Renaissance. Düsseldorf: Schwann.

NIVEN, A. 1985. "Africa and the arts." In: African Affairs, 84, 335, 183–193.

NKETIA, J.H.K. 1979. Die Musik Afrikas. Wilhelmshaven: Heinrichshofen's Verlag.

NKETIA, J.H.K. 1965. Ghana-Music, Dance and Drama. A Review of the Performing Arts of Ghana. Legon, Institute of African Studies.

NKETIA, J.H.K. 1957. "Possession Dances in African Societies." In: Journal of the International Folk Music Council, 9, 4–9.

NZEWI, M. 1971. "The Rhythm of Dance in Iglo Music." In: The Conch, III/2, 104–108.

O'CONNELL, D.C./KOWAL, S./POSNER, R. 1995. Zeichen für Zeit. Tübingen: Gunter Narr.

OPOKU, A.M. 1965. African Dances. University of Ghana, Legon.

PAGER, H. 1989. The Rock Paintings of the upper Brandberg. partI Amis Gorge. Köln: Heinrich-Barth-Institut.

PANTALEONI, H. 1972. "Three Priciples of Timing in Anlo dance drumming." In: African Music, 5, 50ff.

PAUDRAT, J.-L. 1973. African Art of the Dogon. The myths of the cliffs dwellers. New York.

PERROTTET, C. 1988. Ausdruck in Bewegung und Tanz. Bern & Stuttgart: Verlag Paul Haupt.

PETER-BOLANDER, M. 1992. Tanz und Imagination. Paderborn: Jungfermann Verlag.

PIKE, K. 1957. Tone Languages. Ann Arbor: University of Michigan Press.

POMPINO-MARSCHALL, B. 1995. Einführung in die Phonetik. Berlin. Walter de Gruyter.

PRINCE, R. 1982. "The endorphins." In: Ethos, 10, 4, 303–316.

PRINCE, R. 1982(a). "Shamans and Endorphines: Hypotheses for a Synthesis." In: Ethos, 10, 4, 409–423.

QUARCOO, A.K. 1972. "The ancestors in Ghanaian religious and social behaviour." In: Research Review, Dept. of African Studies, University of Ghana, Legon, 8, 2, 1972, 39ff.

RANGER, T.O. 1975. Dance and Society in Eastern Africa 1890–1979: The Beni Ngoma. Berkley: UC Press.

RASMUSSEN, S.J. 1994. "The 'Head Dance', contested self, and art as a balancing act in Tuareg spirit possession." In: Africa, 64, 74–98.

RAY, B.C. 1976. African Religions. Symbol, Ritual, and Community. New Jersey: Prentice-Hall Studies in Religion Series.

REBLING, E. 1989. Die Tanzkunst Indonesiens. Berlin: Henschelverlag.

RIDGEWAY, W. 1915. The Dramas and Dramatic Dances of Non European Races. New York: Cambridge University Press.

ROOD, A.P. "Bété Masked Dance: A view from within." In: African Arts, 2, 3, 36–43.

SADLER, M.E. (ed.). 1935. Arts of West Africa. London: Oxford University Press.

SACHS, C. 1933. World History of the Dance. New York: W. W. Norton & Company.

SAFTIEN, V. 1991. "Vom Totentanz zum Reigen der Seligen." In: Berliner Theologische Zeitschrift, 1, 2–18.

SAUSSURE, F. de. 1967. Grundlagen der Allgemeinen Sprachwissenschaft. Berlin: Walter de Gruyter.

SCHERER, K.R. 1970. Nonverbale Kommunikation. Hamburg: Helmut Buske.

SCHIKOWSKI, J. 1926. Geschichte des Tanzes. Berlin: Büchergilde Gutenberg.

SCHMIDT, J. 1984. Erfahren, was Menschen bewegt – Pina Bausch und das Wuppertaler Tanztheater. Wuppertal.

SCHMIDT-WRENGER, B. 1986. "Music and Dance in Central African Healing Ceremonies." In: M. Honegger/C. Meyer (eds): La musique et le rite Sacré et Profane. Vol. 1. Strasbourg: Association des Publications près les Universités de Strasbourg, 456ff.

SCHWEGER-HEFEL, A. 1970. "Erdherrin und Masken in Sarma." In: Paideuma, XVI, 96–130.

SEBEOK, T.A./UMIKER-SEBEOK, J. (eds.). 1989. The semiotic web. Berlin: Mouton de Gruyter.

SEELIGMANN, S. 1921. Die Zauberkraft des Auges. Den Haag: Couvreuer Verlag

SEGY, L. 1976. Masks of Black Africa. New York: Dover Publications.

SHEETS-JOHNSTONE, M. 1980. The Phenomenology of Dance. New York: Arno Press.

SKENE, R. 1971. Arab and Swahili Dances and Ceremonies. In: Journal of the Royal Anthropological Institute, 47, 413–434.

SLADE, P. 1977. Natural Dance. Developmental Movement and guided action. London: Hodder & Stoughton.

SPENCER, P. 1985. Dance as Antithesis in Samburu discourse. In: P. Spencer (ed.): Society and dance. Cambridge: Cambridge University Press, 140–164.

SPENCER, P. (ed.). 1985(a). Society and the dance. The Social Anthropology of process and performance. London: Cambridge University Press.

SPIETH, J. 1911. Die Religion der Eweer in Süd-Togo. Göttingen: Vandenhoeck und Ruprecht.

STEINER, C. B. 1988. "To dance the spirit." Aspects of African Spirit. Special issue of Chrysalis, 6, 4, 40–43. New York: Swedenborg Foundation.

STRIDE, G.T./IFEKA, C. 1971. Peoples and Empires of West Africa. London: Nelson.

SUDBRACK, J. 1995. "Der Tanz in der Geschichte der christlichen Spiritualität." In: G. Vogler et al., Tanz und Spiritualität. Mainz: Matthias-Grünewald-Verlag, 19–55.

SULZER 1787. Der Tanz.

TAKI, R. 1937. Hachiitu Dance, Ancient Chinese ritual dance and its origin.

THOMAS, H. (ed.). 1993. Dance, Gender and Culture. London: Macmillan Press.

THOMSON, H.J. 1983. "Ingoma – a migrant dance." Paper delivered at a symposium entitled "African Urban Life in Durban in the twentieth Century" at the University of Natal, Durban.

THOMPSON, R.J. 1974. African Art in Motion. Los Angeles: University of California Press.

TIEROU, A. 2014. Alphabet de la danse africaine: méthode Tierou = Alphabet of African dance: Tierou method. Aucamville: C. Rolland.

TRACY, A. 1951. "The Nyanga Panpipe Dance." In: African Music, 73ff.

TRACY, H. 1952. African Dancers of the Witwatersrand Gold Mines. Johannesburg, South Africa: African Music Society.

TRUBETZKOY, N.S. 1939. Grundzüge der Phonologie. Prag.

TURNER, V.W. 1968. The Drums of affliction. A study of Religous Processes among the Ndembu of Zambia. Oxford: Clarendon Press and The International African Institute.

UDOKA, A., n.d. Dance in Nigerian Culture. M.A. Diss. Laban Centre London.

UZUKWU, E.E. 1995. "Körper und Erinnerung in der afrikanischen Liturgie." In: Concilium, 31, 3, 226–232.

VÈRGER, P. 1957. Notes sur la religion Yoruba au Brásil et en Afrique. o. A.

VOGLER, G./SUDBRACK, J./KOHLHAAS, E. 1995. Tanz und Spiritualität. Mainz: Matthias-Grünewald-Verlag.

VOß, J. 1995. "'Von Schritt zu Schritt in verständliche Zeichen und Charactères': Zur Geschichte der Tanznotation." In: Kodikas/Codes. Ars Semeiotica. An International Journal of Semiotics, 18, 1/3, 149–163.

WEBER, Y. 1991. Tanz und Musik in Westafrika. Diplomarbeit Deutsche Sporthochschule, Köln.

WEIDIG, J. 1984. Tanz-Ethnologie. Ahrensburg: Czwalina.

WELSH-ASANTE, K. (ed.). 1996. African Dance: An Artistic, Historical, and Philosophical Inquiry. Trenton & Asmara: Africa World Press.

WESTERMANN, D. 1907. "Zeichensprache des Ewevolkes in Deutsch-Togo." In: MSOS (Mitteilungen des Seminars für Orientalische Sprachen), Abt. 3, 10, 1–14.

WESTERMANN, D. 1902. Archiv der Norddeutschen Mission, Depositum des Staatsarchivs, Bremen. 7.1020.

WIGMAN, M. 1963. Die Sprache des Tanzes. Stuttgart: Ernst Battenberg.

WIGMAN, M. 1933. "The philosophy of modern dance." In: Europa, 1, 1.

WILCOX, S. 1992. The Phonetics of Fingerspelling. Amsterdam & Philadelphia: John Benjamins Publishing Company.

WILLIAMS, D. 1978. "Deep Structures of the Dance." In: Yearbook of Symbolic Anthropology, 1.

YARTEY, N. 1992. Dances in Ghana. Accra.

ZELEZA, P.T. (ed.). 2003. Leisure in Urban Africa. Trenton, N.J.: Africa World Press.

van ZILE, J. 1988. "Examining movement in the context of the music event: a working model." In: D. Christensen (ed): 1988 Yearbook for Traditional Music. New York: Cambridge University Press.

van ZILE, J. 1976. Dance in Africa, Asia, and the Pacific. New York: MSS Information Corp.